PRAISE FOR

Bringing Your Business to Life

You don't often read about prudence, justice, courage and temperance in the business literature, but they are the virtues that set the truly great entrepreneurs apart from all the rest. If you want to be one of them, you need to read this book. Jeffrey Cornwall and Michael Naughton have done a masterful job of illuminating a side of business we all should be thinking about.

Bo Burlingham
Editor-at-large, *Inc.*
Author, *Small Giants: Companies that Choose to Be Great Instead of Big*

While reading *Bringing Your Business to Life*, I found multiple opportunities to apply the Four Virtues to my life and to the ventures that I'm presently involved with. This book is practical, insightful and relevant for entrepreneurs who desire to better understand the social, spiritual and economic impact we can have through our for-profit and nonprofit endeavors.

Corey Cleek
General Editor, *Devotional Ventures*

Jeff Cornwall and Michael Naughton have created a compelling argument for the integration of ethical and moral behavior and entrepreneurship. They dispel the myth that the "Ethical Entrepreneur" is an oxymoron; rather they offer strong evidence that success and entrepreneurship are not mutually exclusive. *Bringing Your Business to Life* offers a vehicle for more cross-campus collaboration by introducing liberal arts concepts into the phenomena known as the entrepreneur and entrepreneurship.

George T. Solomon, D.B.A.
Director, Center for Entrepreneurial Excellence
The George Washington University

Bringing Your Business to Life is a prescription for success in life as well as in business. It is a great synopsis of how financial and spiritual well-being can intersect in doing well by doing good. It reveals that it is not only what we do as a chosen profession, but it is who we are as a person that will dictate where we go in life. This book also acknowledges that even though mistakes will inevitably be made as we sometimes fail our way to success, with values and virtues as the pillars of our foundation for building an integrated personal and professional life, those mistakes should be mistakes of the head and not of the heart. *Bringing Your Business to Life* is good medicine for good business. In fact, it reminds us that doing the right thing and putting faith into action is the best medicine for a great life.

Ron Loeppke, MD, MPH, FACPM, FACOEM

Bringing Your Business to Life helps fill a real gap in the literature on and for entrepreneurs (and by extension, on and for business). It bridges two worlds that have not spoken to each other in our culture as much as we need—the world of ethics and morality and religion on one side and the world of capitalism and business and entrepreneurship on the other. It provides a valuable framework for thinking about and practicing ethical entrepreneurship and for helping us see how to go beyond a limited, values-free, amoral, profits-are-the-only-measure-of-success view of business. *Bringing Your Business to Life* gives us essential tools that we can use to build entrepreneurial ventures—and entrepreneurial lives—that matter and make a difference.

John Wark
Consultant and Former Software CEO

Professors Cornwall and Naughton utilize real-life experiences to demonstrate that entrepreneurship is a virtuous profession. Using basic Christian principles, the authors explore the issues facing entrepreneurs during all stages of their venture and challenge the myth that entrepreneurs have to act in unethical ways to survive. This is a must-read for anyone starting a new business, and it is a great primer for a class in entrepreneurial ethics.

Jeffrey S. Hornsby, Ph.D., SPHR
Jack Vanier Chair of Innovation and Entrepreneurship
Kansas State University

Tired of conventional commentary regarding entrepreneurship? Join a conversation with a wise theologian and a reflective business founder who share stories and perspectives from a seven-year dialogue. Together they examine the charisma of the entrepreneur through the lens of Christian virtues, suggesting a deep spirituality particular to the calling of those who drive our most dynamic business sector. This is a wise, readable and formative essay that will stick to the memory of any reader concerned with contemporary wealth formation through start-up enterprise.

Andre L. Delbecq
Thomas J. and Kathleen L. McCarthy University
Professor, Leavey School of Business, Santa Clara University, and the
Professor and Director of the Institute for Spirituality and Organizational
Leadership at the Santa Clara University School of Business

Bringing Your Business *to* Life

THE FOUR VIRTUES THAT WILL HELP YOU BUILD A BETTER BUSINESS—AND A BETTER LIFE

Jeffrey Cornwall
Michael Naughton

Regal

From Gospel Light
Ventura, California, U.S.A.

Published by Regal
From Gospel Light
Ventura, California, U.S.A.
www.regalbooks.com
Printed in the U.S.A.

Library of Congress Cataloging-in-Publication Data
Cornwall, Jeffrey R.
Bringing your business to life : the four virtues that will help you build a
better business and a better life / Jeffrey Cornwall, Michael Naughton.
p. cm.
Includes bibliographical references.
ISBN 978-0-8307-4593-7 (hard cover)
1. Business—Religious aspects—Christianity. I. Naughton, Michael. II. Title.
HF5388.C667 2008
261.8'5—dc22
2008007497

1 2 3 4 5 6 7 8 9 10 11 12 13 14 15 / 15 14 13 12 11 10 09 08

Rights for publishing this book outside the U.S.A. or in non-English languages are
administered by Gospel Light Worldwide, an international not-for-profit ministry.
For additional information, please visit www.glww.org, email info@glww.org, or write
to Gospel Light Worldwide, 1957 Eastman Avenue, Ventura, CA 93003, U.S.A.

THIS BOOK IS DEDICATED TO
OUR FATHERS,
ROBERT CORNWALL AND NOEL NAUGHTON,
BOTH GOOD ENTREPRENEURS.

Contents

The Challenge of Being a Good Entrepreneur

Jeffrey Cornwall and Michael Naughton explore four virtues for building a good company. They examine the impact of our changing culture and the opportunities that new entrepreneurs have, provided they have fresh ideas and good business plans. This book, *Bringing Your Business to Life*, explores the fact that oftentimes much more than a fresh approach and a good business plan are needed to strengthen the opportunities for success within an entrepreneurial business environment.

In order to succeed as an entrepreneur in a business climate that has not historically supported small businesses on a long-term basis, the entrepreneur must focus inward on his employees and value them as much as he values his final product and profit margins. *Bringing Your Business to Life* examines the use of a holistic approach, an essential attribute of a successful business. An entrepreneur who attempts to run his or her business by focusing on and supporting the "whole" employee will create a business environment with higher morale, and in turn, higher collaboration and overall productivity. The importance of having the whole person in the office requires the realization that employees have health concerns, family concerns, personal issues, motivational issues and the obvious communication and confrontational issues that exist within every business.

For example, an employee can be extremely professional in terms of his or her job performance, yet at the same time alienate fellow workers by not understanding the needs and concerns that other employees are experiencing in their business and personal lives. Each business develops a culture of its own, and no matter how good its product is, the business will not maintain the best employees without understanding that in addition to the professionalism of each individual, there is a social, personal and often a spiritual aspect of each person's life that has to be understood and accepted if we want the whole person to be committed to the goals and challenges of the overall business.

Because of the fact that Curb Records started from scratch, almost 45 years ago, I'm proud that this company continues to be the oldest record company that has not changed ownership. Nevertheless, as this book suggests, it will take the vision and new ideas from the next generation if this company is to survive in the future, and I'm proud that my daughter Courtney Curb Childress, who is now an executive with Curb Records, has been asked to contribute her thoughts to this foreword.

> Many people may base my father's unprecedented success on hit records and his musical genius, but his success has evolved from more than simply the musical "product" that the company produces. Listening to him on phone calls from the time I was a little girl sitting on his lap to now, on the other end of a conference call as his Director of Human Resources, I have only heard him

value employees and use what we now refer to as the holistic model. His conversation with an employee will range from fast-paced music chart standings and business strategies to discussions of ailing pets or family issues such as elder parents in need of medical care. I remember attending employee weddings with my father as a child. And just this past month, he spent the day visiting an employee's father in the hospital to make sure he was being treated with the best care and to be sure his employee had the support she needed. Even in the midst of schedules with back-to-back meetings and conference calls, my father finds time to talk to his employees and make sure they are "whole" when they come into the office. Furthermore, if an employee is suffering from a personal problem, my father has created a company culture that will assist in solving any employee issue, regardless of its relevance to the music business.

When we realize that most new jobs are being created by new business models, we need to examine the practices of other cultures with high employee productivity, such as Japan, and other Asian countries. For example, many of the businesses in these countries provide time for employee exercise programs, counseling programs, continuing education support, as well as support for many of the personal needs of employees, particularly those with responsibilities for children or elderly family members. It is absolutely clear that an employee's health and other personal pressures are a major factor in terms of creating a positive business environment and achieving positive productivity. This approach has worked for years in other countries, but often is difficult to implement in our domestic business culture where many employees determine their value to a company solely by the base salary, coupled with raises and bonuses. Younger employees often would prefer to not even have medical benefits if it impacts their salary. For this reason, the challenge of explaining the value of these long-term benefits as opposed to short-term salary gains is one of the major difficulties facing this approach.

The new generation of workers that will be entering the workforce in the next decade has been reared and educated with more opportunities than any generation before them. The more that young entrepreneurs can learn to embrace a balanced work-life ratio, while incorporating virtue and holistic thinking into their business model, the better chance their small businesses will stand to succeed.

Mike Curb
Founder, Curb Records

Acknowledgments

There are several sources of people who have made this book possible. First, we are indebted to our students, who have engaged this crossroad of entrepreneurship and the virtues with a great deal of honesty, interest and at times skepticism. In the classroom, these young men and women have been alive, vibrant and full of inquiry, enhancing our own understanding of the topic.

In the last 10 years, we have also talked with many entrepreneurs and organizational leaders, many of whom are mentioned in this book. They were generous with their time, which was one of their scarcest resources. While we cannot mention all of them, we would like to thank the following for their insight and critique: Anthony Brenninkmeyer, Bill Brinkman, Dan Crockett, Jean Loup Dherse, Charles Hagood, Jason Hartwell, Tom Henry, Joe Keeley, Clyde Lear, William Lee, Ed Mosel, Robert Ouimet, Jerry Rick, Greg Schiffer, Dr. James Stefansic, Bob Wahlstedt, Thom Winninger and Luke Wooten.

We also talked with many of our academic colleagues about the virtues. We are especially indebted to Robert Kennedy, who challenged us throughout the writing of this book to be more precise in our use of the virtues. We are also grateful for the comments throughout the years from Helen Alford, Tom Bausch, Don Briel, Dick Broholm, Jeanne Buckeye, Bill Cavanaugh, Steve Cortright, Andre Delbecq, Jim Emrich, Jack Fortin,

Ken Goodpaster, John Haughey, Dean Maines, Dennis McCann, John McVea, Ernest Pierucci, Deborah Savage, David Specht, Brian Shapiro, Michael Stebbins, Chris Thompson, Bill Toth, as well as others whose conversations formed our understanding of the virtue tradition.

Of course, the virtue tradition is not only an intellectual tradition but also a lived one, and we are grateful for our parents, siblings, wives and children who have formed us in the virtues and challenged our vices. Finally, we are grateful to all those who helped in the logistics of putting this book together: Erin Anderson and Chris Gray, for their help with many of the interviews with entrepreneurs, and Mary Kay O'Rourke, Becky Gann, Chris Gray, Josh Grinolds and Erin Dolan for their editing.

Introduction

God has created me to do him some definite service; He has committed some work to me which he has not committed to another. I have my mission. I may never know it in this life but I shall be told it in the next. . . . I am a link in a chain, a bond of connection between persons. He has not created me for nothing.

JOHN HENRY NEWMAN

In 2000, we began team teaching a theology course on faith and entrepreneurship. The course was an instant success among the entrepreneurship students at the University of St. Thomas, Minnesota. In 2002, the course received the National Outstanding Course Award from the United States Association for Small Business and Entrepreneurship. We felt that we were on to something that was, for the most part, repressed by mainstream culture and ignored by the church. Mainstream culture was uncomfortable talking about how faith relates to the work of entrepreneurs in their businesses. The church seemed to have little interest in examining how being good can be a part of being in business.

Students reported that they were attracted to the course because it was one of the few times in their college tenure when they encountered an attempt to integrate the themes of their liberal arts education with their business major. The course focused on the integration of faith and reason, vocation and

17

work, the spiritual and the material, virtue and skill, and principles and policies. This engagement was at the same time theologically grounded in the Christian tradition and seriously engaged in the practical and complex matters of running a company. We have also talked to a lot of entrepreneurs in the last 10 years who are searching for ways to integrate their faith, their values and their entrepreneurial spirit in their work. They are not interested in a simplistic approach to integrating faith and work that results in proselytizing their employees, customers and suppliers, nor are they interested in a moral and spiritual light approach that dwindles their faith to a mere guarantee for success.

These students and entrepreneurs realize that there are more choices to faith and work than a secularism that reduces faith to private opinion or to a false evangelism that fails to respect the freedom of others. They want to be able to speak and live from the center of their faith, but they also want to be sure that the people they work with are able to do the same.

Bringing Your Business to Life provides an alternative by drawing upon the virtue tradition that has been nurtured and developed for over 3,000 years. It avoids the trappings of a morally light approach. While sophisticated in the technical understanding of entrepreneurship, too many books are surprisingly simplistic on the moral complexity of starting and growing an enterprise. In a similar way, books on the moral and spiritual life are naïve on the difficulties and pressures of running a business. This book draws upon a rich and profound tradition of the virtues and is grounded in extensive interviews with entrepreneurs who share their experiences of struggling with how to be faithful within their businesses.

One of the surprises of our work together came when Jeff, who ran his own company for several years, was first exposed to the virtue tradition. He was struck by its explanatory power. Rather than confusing the practical, he saw that the virtue tradition within Christianity and Western civilization helped him understand more deeply his own experience as an entrepreneur. It was like discovering that he had been speaking prose all his life without knowing it. Jeff came to the realization that his actions were either good or bad habits, that is, either virtues or vices, and that if he had come to this insight earlier, he may have made better decisions throughout his life, not only as an entrepreneur but also as a husband, father and church member.

The virtues as well as the vices not only explained more clearly what was actually happening in Jeff's work and in him, but the virtues actually brought *life* to his business by connecting him with others and with God. T. S. Eliot captures this kind of life in his poem *Chorus on the Rock*:

> *What life have you if you have not life together?*
> *There is no life that is not in community,*
> *And no community not lived in praise of God.*

Jeff and many of the entrepreneurs we interview in this book reveal for us that when they are at their best, when they feel connected and full of life in their companies, they are often describing a pattern that we call virtue. And the principal characteristics of *bringing their business to life* center in strengthening bonds of communion with their employees, customers and investors, and with God. These virtues, these bonds of connection, build simultaneously both a better business *and* a better life.

Yet, while we had a strong sense of the importance of virtue in entrepreneurship, very little had been written on the subject. It became clear to both of us that entrepreneurs and the discipline of entrepreneurship had a lot to learn from Scripture, Aristotle, Augustine, Aquinas, C. S. Lewis, Gilbert Meilaender, Josef Pieper, Alasdair MacIntyre, Stanley Hauerwas, Servais Pinckaers, Jean Porter, and a host of others who have written on the importance of virtue. What Mike found so striking, however, was how little the Christian and Western tradition connected this profound wisdom of virtue to business and entrepreneurship. How unfortunate it was that theologians and philosophers were not constructively connecting the virtues of prudence, justice, courage and temperance to the practical realities of running a business.

Since teaching our first course eight years ago, we have been working together to integrate business practice and theory with a faith-filled vision that provides a powerful integration. We have written several articles together, presented papers both nationally and internationally, and have given dozens of talks to entrepreneurs and business leaders. Our diverse backgrounds provide a complementarity between theory and practice, scholarship and experience and theology and business.

Bringing Your Business to Life is the synthesis of our work together. The book examines the virtues necessary for *being good,* within the complexities of the life of running a business. The book is a unique blend of real entrepreneurial cases and practical insights of the virtue tradition. *Bringing Your Business to Life* provides principles, practices and stories that display the virtues necessary for business to contribute to a *good life* overall.

A Look Ahead

The book is divided into three parts. In Part One, we introduce the reader to the larger issue of faith and entrepreneurship and why this topic is so important at this time in our history. Chapter 1 takes a serious look at how entrepreneurs and leaders strive to create a tradition within their businesses in which the good business they create can be passed along to help better our economy and our culture. Entrepreneurial firms have the capacity to be a great force for good, so long as they are connected to a robust culture that prepares them for the challenges of running a business.

Chapter 2 introduces the "two Vs"—vocation and virtue. The chapter explores the problem of the *divided life*, and suggests a remedy to the divided life, namely, a *vocation* and the particular habits that embody a vocation—the *cardinal virtues* (prudence, justice, courage and temperance).

In Part Two, we examine the specific virtues of prudence, justice, courage and temperance in the context of the entrepreneurial journey. Chapter 3 explores the importance of prudence to the entrepreneur. The prudent entrepreneur is not to be seen as cunning and opportunistic, the tactician, who by concealing her real intentions, deceives others in achieving her self-centered goals. Rather, she is a person who has the necessary entrepreneurial skills, perceives the situation as it is, and directs her activity toward greater ends that multiply the resources of the world. She is a good steward, often using a variety of bootstrapping techniques to make the most of the resources she has available to her. She is not a "taker" from the resources of the world, but a contributor. We focus on how prudence connects effective means to good ends in the right circumstances.

Chapter 4 confronts the entrepreneur's suspicion of the virtue of justice. He tends to be suspicious of justice largely because it is so often understood as externally imposed constraints by the government and other forces. In this chapter, we focus on the meaning of justice within the Christian tradition and examine one company's struggle to establish right relationships from its founding through its compensation system. We show that justice is not some restraint imposed on the company, but a natural reality that needs to be named for what it is—a search for right relationships that creates a community of work. Justice may not be the first virtue that comes to mind when we think of the entrepreneur, but, by creating right relationships with the stakeholders of the business, it should be.

In chapter 5, we examine the relationship between risk-taking and the virtue of courage. Entrepreneurs usually begin their businesses with a great vision, but soon find themselves overwhelmed by adversity. They are tempted to restrict their concerns to survival issues and retreat from the difficulties of a grander vision for the enterprise. While entrepreneurs will acknowledge feelings of being overwhelmed, they rarely describe them as temptations of retreat, of fear, of being vulnerable. This chapter names these fears, doubts and temptations, and explores how the virtue of courage can be a response to such difficulties.

Chapter 6 challenges the entrepreneur to take seriously the importance of temperance, recognizing when enough is enough. Many entrepreneurs find that their work brings out a certain flow, a rhythm, a certain sense of being connected and alive, that other activities don't seem to give. Their work often brings a great deal of pleasure, satisfaction and self-esteem. Yet when does an entrepreneur's desire to make his enterprise successful cross the line from being a healthy passion to achieve something, to an addiction that disorders other important aspects of her life? One of the more difficult challenges for an entrepreneur is to recognize when enough is enough. It is precisely the pleasure of the work that can lead entrepreneurs into the temptation to disorder all other important things in life, such as marriage, family, health, friendships and religion. This chapter examines this disease of workaholism in the entrepreneur and prescribes important practices of temperance that can resist its spread.

Finally, in Section Three, we provide a way of "seeing things whole." In this final chapter we help the reader look at the organization as a whole, to see things whole, and we summarize the practices of the good entrepreneur who aspires to build a company faithful to the virtues. All of the virtues discussed in this book interact and complement each other in every situation an entrepreneur faces. However, there are pressures that all entrepreneurs face as their businesses grow, that create pressures to drift away from their commitment to build a faithful company. This chapter reveals a holistic understanding of the enterprise that helps entrepreneurs see how particular practices fit within the whole life of the organization, and how to bring all of the virtues together to bring *life* to business.

PART ONE

The Good Entrepreneur

1

Tradition:
Passing It On

Tradition means giving votes to the most obscure of all classes,
our ancestors. It is the democracy of the dead. Tradition refuses to
submit to the small and arrogant oligarchy of those who merely
happen to be walking about. All democrats object to men being
disqualified by the accident of birth; tradition objects to their
being disqualified by the accident of death.

G. K. CHESTERTON

One of the more tragic scenes in American film is found in *Gladiator* when Caesar (Richard Harris), who is growing old, has to choose his successor to Rome. He has come to the heart-rending realization that his own son, Commodus (Joaquin Phoenix), is too corrupt to lead Rome. Caesar informs his son that he will give his rule to Maximus (Russell Crowe), the good and virtuous general. Devastated by the news, Commodus's response confirms Caesar's judgment:

> You wrote to me once, listing the four chief virtues.
> Wisdom, Justice, Fortitude and Temperance. As I read the
> list I knew I had none of them. But I have other virtues,

father. Ambition, that can be a virtue when it drives us to excel. Resourcefulness. Courage. Perhaps not on the battlefield but there are many forms of courage. Devotion, to my family, to you. But none of my virtues were on your list.

Overwhelmed with sadness by his son's inability to connect the four cardinal virtues to the good of the community, Caesar confesses to Commodus: "Your fault as a son is my failure as a father." Caesar, the father, who has conquered many lands, did not conquer the small-mindedness of his own son's vision of the good. His failure as a father to pass on the virtues of wisdom, justice, fortitude and temperance to his own child was also a failure of his own leadership, since it was these cardinal virtues of the next generation on which the greatness of Rome depended.

This scene raises many important questions for us today. What virtues are we passing on to our children? If our country is to be great, we have to pass on to the next generation of leaders not only property, institutions, resources, skills and knowledge, but most importantly virtues, and in particular the cardinal virtues, those virtues that develop the emotional, social and spiritual dimensions of our personhood.

Yet, increasingly it seems, our language, our education and our principles have made this holistic development of the person more difficult. David Brooks, in interviews with students from Princeton University, described them as "lively conversationalists on just about any topic—except moral argument and character-building."[1] He explains that while their "parents impose all sorts of rules to reduce safety risks and encourage achievement, they do not go to great lengths to build character, the way adults and adult institutions did a century ago. . . . When it comes to character and virtue, these young people have been left on their own."[2]

Like Caesar, we may have great achievements in our life. We may have conquered markets, introduced technical innovations, built enterprises and accumulated great wealth, but we may be failing in one of the most important tasks of our culture—the passing on of a moral tradition that builds good character in our children and that contributes to a great country.

The Impact of Small Giants on Tradition

This challenge of what we pass on to our children is particularly seen in one of the most important social forces in America today: entrepreneurship. Entrepreneurs are a powerful force in our society because they create trends, break molds and cause significant changes within society. Throughout our economic history, they are the ones who have helped build and transform our economy from the industrial age, to the age of mass production, to the information age and to whatever our economic future may hold.

In addition to the many positive contributions they have made to our economy and our culture, entrepreneurs have also started the massive pornography industry on the Internet, violent video games, investment scams and other superfluous products and services. These positive and negative realities within our society were not started by the government or by multinationals, although some are now imitating these realities, but by individuals and small groups of people, what Bo Burlingham has described as "small giants."[3]

Entrepreneurs and the businesses they have created are having a major impact on the world in terms of what they are passing on. To think otherwise is to ignore some significant facts. According to recent statistics from the United States Small Business Administration:

- Total employment by Fortune 500 companies has dropped from 20 percent of the U.S. workforce in 1980, to about 7 percent in the late 1990s, with the Fortune 500 losing 5 million jobs over the past 20 years.

- Entrepreneurs create more jobs than were being lost by the Fortune 500, resulting in a steady growth in employment since the 1970s, creating 77 percent of the new jobs created in the past two decades.

- In the mid-twentieth century, about 200,000 new businesses were started each year in the United States. That number is now estimated to be 650,000 new businesses started each year.

- It is estimated that there are now over 23 million small businesses in the U.S., and they represent over 50 percent of the GDP (Gross Domestic Product), over 50 percent of total employment and 45 percent of total U.S. payroll.

- Despite the general misconception that new ventures fail at a high rate, studies reveal that entrepreneurial businesses in the U.S. survive for at least five years at a rate of 45 to 50 percent.

- U.S. small businesses create 67 percent of all new innovations, 95 percent of all radical innovations, and 14 times more patents per employee than large patenting firms.

- Recent studies find that 97 percent of all exports from the U.S. come from small businesses and these represent 29 percent of all export value.[4]

It is clear that at the dawn of the twenty-first century we are in the beginning of a new economic wave dominated by new entrepreneurial ventures. The question we face as entrepreneurs and businesspeople is this: What are we passing on through our businesses to our children, our community and our culture?

In his discussions with entrepreneurs from Silicon Valley, Andre Delbecq asks what defines their success. Similar to the responses Jim Collins received in his book *Good to Great*, their answers are not about survival or income or margin, but the quality of the company they pass on. They obviously want to pass on profitable and efficient companies that will survive well beyond them. But survival is not enough for them. They want their companies to flourish after they are gone, just as parents would want their children to flourish after they are gone. As leaders, they work so that their companies can live *better* after they leave.

Difficulty of Passing on the Good in Business

But this task of "passing on" is not easy. Only a small number of family businesses make it to the third generation, and only a few entrepreneurial companies are able to carry on their original mission. We will explore the challenges of building and passing on good companies throughout this book from the stories of several entrepreneurs, including those of one of the authors, Jeff Cornwall.[5] In 1988, I (Jeff) started, with two other partners, a series of health-care provider companies that eventually became Atlantic Behavioral Health Systems. This was a boom time in health care in the United States. Managed care had just started to begin its transformation of how health care would be provided and how it would be paid for. We saw an opportunity to build a company that took full advantage of the changes occurring in the industry.

As care became managed, insurance companies were seeking alternative forms of treatment and treatment protocols that had two fundamental characteristics: better outcomes and lower costs. In the mental health segment of the industry we believed that this would create the need for treatment facilities that could provide alternatives to the long hospitalizations that were the standard course of treatment at that time. These long hospital stays were proving to be ineffective (high rates of readmission were very common, especially among adolescent patients) and very costly, with daily costs ranging as high as $1,000 to $2,000 per day, with stays that were often measured in weeks and even months. We planned to bring innovative treatment programs and protocol to the private insurance market from the public mental health market where limited budgets had always been a fact of life.

All three of us had committed from the very beginning of our partnership to create a health-care business that was different from many that we had seen in this rapidly evolving industry.

We focused on three main areas that we wanted to be the foundation of our culture: commitment to our employees, a focus on quality care ahead of any concern for profits, and market leadership in innovation. We wanted to build an enduring organization that maintained this culture indefinitely, regardless of our roles. A good number of health-care companies had been created during this time that clearly had only one objective: profit maximization. Wall Street and venture capital monies were flowing freely into start-up health-care ventures. While we all wanted to make a profit, we also wanted to build a company that we could be proud of.

Rather than rely on frequent layoffs and downsizings to generate the highest levels of profits possible, we wanted to build a business that created jobs that people could rely on. We viewed our commitment to employees as a long-term relationship, and we intended to do our best to demonstrate this through our actions. We considered each and every hire very seriously. Was this a position that we could fund over the long-term through the growth in the business? We never wanted to hire for a new position unless we were confident that the person we hired could rely on that job to provide for their livelihood as long as they performed their work to the best of their abilities.

We also agreed that we wanted to create a patient-focused culture in our business. A common practice at that time was to discharge a patient as soon as insurance coverage ran out, even if it risked the patient losing any ground that had been gained to that point in their treatment. Although we had to follow sound business practices and ensure a healthy cash flow for the survival of our new venture, we also wanted to be known as a company that did not put profits ahead of patient care. So, for example, if a patient's insurance coverage was no longer going to pay for treatment in one of our facilities, we would aggressively seek alternative treatment settings for that patient. But if it took a week or two after their insurance coverage ran out to find the right placement, we would provide treatment through the transition even if we knew that payment would be unlikely.

Finally, we wanted to be known as a leader in innovation. We gained great satisfaction from seeking a problem in the market and creating a new program or a new business that turned that problem into an opportunity. One of our greatest measures of success was our ability to meet the evolving needs within our segment of a rapidly changing health-care industry. We believed that such innovation would help contribute to creating a better health-care system out of the disruption, uncertainty and even chaos that the rapid changes in health care brought about by managed care.

During our early growth, our approach seemed to work very well. In a relatively short period of time, we grew from a handful of employees in a single location, to hundreds of employees working in several facilities across the state of North Carolina. But this market success also created unintended changes in our company. One day while one of my partners and I were going over some routine issues over a cup of coffee, out of nowhere, or so it seemed to me at the time, he made a profound statement: "I hardly recognize this business anymore. It is no longer the kind of place it was when we first started." At first I dismissed his comment. Our company had seen great market success and I was too busy trying to keep up with all of our growing pains to worry about his nostalgic musings.

But as I reflected further on what he said to me, I began to realize that he was right. Our business that was formed based on the intent to have a culture that would be innovative, flexible, supportive, and employee and customer centered, had become bureaucratic, unresponsive and even somewhat of a cold place to work. The culture had drifted away from what we had intended. The change was slow and even imperceptible, but the outcome was clear—our identity had fundamentally changed over the period of about three years of rapid growth. And these unintended changes were starting to erode the foundations of our business. Customers were no longer looking to us for innovative solutions, and staff turnover was increasing. It seemed the best customers and the best employees perceived these changes before we did, and they were letting us know by moving their business elsewhere and by taking new jobs.

We were forced to address several critical questions: What had happened to our business? How did this change happen? Were these changes the inevitable outcome of our growth and success? What had we done, and failed to do, that caused our culture to drift so far from where it began? Was it possible to regain the culture that we had originally intended for our business? Will it be possible to find a means to ensure that the kind of business we created can be sustained into the future, even if we are no longer the owners?

Although the growth of a business is one cause of such fundamental challenges as we experienced in our business, there are other types of transitions in private ventures that can also drift a business away from its original culture and the founding values instilled by the entrepreneurs who formed the business. When J. Robert Ouimet from Montreal, Quebec, sold one of his food processing companies to his youngest son, he was looking forward to passing on a legacy of doing business that he received from his father. Both J. Robert and his father sought a deeper integration of faith and running a business, and developed a series of management practices that would harmonize spiritual and human values with the economic demands for productivity and profits (we will discuss some of these later in the book). This effort grew out of J. Robert's desire to more profoundly connect his faith and his vocation as a business leader so that his company would be a place where people could develop their abilities and talents and bring their whole selves to work. His youngest son, however, as soon as he took ownership, disowned this legacy. As he put it, "I consider religion to be a personal choice that has no place in the management of a commercial enterprise." For J. Robert, this fracture caused by his son was one of the most significant moments of suffering in his life.

What Good Do We Pass On?

These two particular stories should raise for entrepreneurs and leaders in business a serious question: *What good am I passing on within my company?* Of course, we can't pass on goods that we do not have. As the Latin proverb puts it, *nemo dat quod non habet*: "Nobody gives what he does not have." The good we wish to pass on is a good that must be part of us.

So who is a *good entrepreneur* and what exactly makes such a person *good*? For some people, this question will strike a tone of presumption. You can almost hear the responses: "Who are you to determine what is good?" "Who are you to say who is virtuous?" "Who are you to tell anyone how they should work and live?" Certainly all of us are always in danger of becoming too smug, too self-righteous, too judgmental and too full of ourselves to realize that we may not have all the right answers. We know too many entrepreneurs and businesspeople, and many who claim to be Christian, who think that they are quite good but whose employees and customers would think otherwise. Our hearts can become too fat with our own self-perceived goodness that we impose on others.

When we speak of "the good," we don't mean not quite excellent or being mediocre. What we mean by the good is that moral quality of character that perfects us as human beings, that makes us who we should be, who we were created to be. This is why we have to face the fact that these questions of goodness and virtue provide no neutral ground, no fence-sitting. Any attempt to escape moral argument of the good leads to what philosophers call the self-referential contradiction: Not to define is to define; not to claim moral truth is a moral claim; not to judge is a judgment; not to have universal beliefs is a universal belief. We cannot get away from making moral judgments, precisely because we, as human beings, are inherently moral and spiritual by nature. If we are honest with ourselves, we see that each one of us has a moral and spiritual perspective on what we define as good work and the virtues associated with that work. The sooner we are clear on this, the better off we will be in the long run in having our work developing us into the people we are supposed to be.

When business literature takes up the question of what makes the entrepreneur good, they tend to focus on their enormous creativity, innovation and wealth-generating ability. It emphasizes their skills and characteristics, habits if you will, that some people describe as "entrepreneurial virtues." These virtues focus on the habits that generate and accumulate wealth: ambition, ingenuity, diligence, perseverance, tenacity and self-discipline. While entrepreneurial virtues are necessary for successful enterprises, they ignore the deeper question of the good that we want to explore in this book: For what *purpose* do I create wealth—myself, family, investors, the common*wealth*? Entrepreneurial virtues can be exercised in new ways to fight cancer or market tobacco, in producing insightful historical documentaries or creating pornographic films. Even someone like Jim Collins, whose work on leadership is some of the best in the field, lists among his great leaders Joseph F. Cullman III, CEO of Philip Morris, whose company produces a cancer-causing, addictive product largely marketed to the young and now developing world countries. If this is now greatness, we will stick to the good.

There is something deeper here that business literature is not getting to. The entrepreneur's capacity to create wealth always faces the question: *For what?* For all the technical and skillful advances we can make in creating wealth, the techniques and skills do not answer the question of whether they make us truly better off or not. While income statements and balance sheets may tell us that we have created more wealth than last year, and technological advances may increase productivity and enhance market share, they do not tell us if we are better for it. In other words, the question of whether our creative entrepreneurial impulses lead to authentic *human* development cannot be fully understood within accounting, finance, marketing or operations. Business disciplines do not have moral and spiritual resources to answer whether we are becoming more or less human.

If we are to get beyond the rather superficial understanding of what is great, we need to draw upon a moral tradition that is deeper and wiser than what business literature too often gives us. That tradition is Christianity. Contrary to what J. Robert Ouimet's son stated above, the Christian religion is not a private affair. It is very concerned about people's work, not in terms of proselytizing and *imposing* religion on others, but rather *proposing* a vision of how work can develop people.

This book challenges entrepreneurs and businesspeople to examine what we call the "two Vs": *vocation* and *virtue*. Deep within each one of us is a calling to do great things in this world, which is embodied through a set of habits that we call the four cardinal virtues of prudence, justice, courage and temperance. This vision of work is mostly absent from the current literature available to entrepreneurs and businesspeople. Yet, without a sense of vocation along with the virtues, we believe that businesses will produce more people like the corrupt Commodus than the virtuous Maximus. We have seen too many entrepreneurs and businesspeople morally and spiritually unprepared for the financial and psychological pressures they encounter in business. They naively thought that if they had the right technical skills and financial know-how, then all would be well.

But not all is well. The last 10 years have revealed in rather dramatic ways the moral instability of business. The moral collapse of the dot-coms, Enron, WorldCom and others were for the most part not caused by vicious people, but by technically skilled and financially knowledgeable people who lost sight of any moral norms in their attempts to achieve their economic goals. Without a rich understanding of the moral and spiritual implications of what people do in their businesses, they misunderstand their contribution to the wider society and ultimately lose perspective of their very selves.

Culture: Seeing Things Whole

At the heart of our book is a belief, which our experience confirms, that all the business skills and all the government policies, while important and necessary, will not make a good company or a good entrepreneur. Neither markets nor the state by themselves have this capacity. The source of goodness will primarily come from the culture and its institutions and not primarily from the market or the state. Without a strong culture, the state tends toward totalitarianism and the market tends toward consumerism and careerism.

If culture is so important, then, what do we mean by this word? "Culture," as the root of the word indicates, *cultivates* within us a way of seeing the world, to see what is real, to make sense of reality. It creates in us sensitivities to what is important and worthy of sacrifice. Jeff and his partners were willing to take great personal and financial risk to build their business. But they did not perceive that financial gain alone would make taking such risks worthwhile. J. Robert Ouimet had built a business not only to create wealth for his family but also to create a faith-based business that would span generations of his family. These entrepreneurs and others like them were influenced by the cultural institutions of family, church and school. This larger culture formed within them a vision of the good that described what they saw as most worthy in their lives and in their businesses. This cultural formation helps entrepreneurs to discern through all the data, all the ideas, all the alternatives, and land on what counts in life and how that will play out in the businesses they create and build.

When culture is at its best, that is, when it connects us to our created purpose, to our true nature, to our destiny, it enables us to see the whole and not merely the parts. Culture allows us to receive the whole of creation, and helps us realize our role within it. This wholeness is arrived at by connecting us to the fundamental events of our life—birth, death, work, love—in such a way that these events are related in an organic whole rather than in an isolated, compartmentalized fashion.

This is why at the heart of every culture worthy of the name, including the culture of the businesses we create, is a *religious* question. The word itself, *religio,* means to reconnect—to help us reintegrate that which has become divided. It is also why tradition is often connected to religion. In order to reconnect, religion seeks to pass on that which reconnects us with ourselves, with others and with God.

More concretely, culture is a common way of life. It has a tradition and it is embodied in particular institutions that are informed by moral and spiritual principles. Those institutions that have the best chance to help us see holistically and the capacity to sink deep within us virtues, that is, good habits that direct us to the end for which we were created, are family, education and religion. Many of these institutions, however, when they are at their best are not generic institutions. They do not convey to their members only a universal ethic of being good. They are most vibrant when they are most specific, and this is precisely why in this book we will draw specifically on the Christian religion in examining vocation and the virtues for the good entrepreneur.

Using a particular religious focus makes some people nervous. They are concerned that religious perspectives will lead to irresolvable conflicts, intolerance, proselytism and even religious wars. But what should make people more nervous, particularly in our culture today, is the belief that we can handle the challenges of this new entrepreneurial economy with only economic and political resources. While we must always be mindful of the worst abuses of religion—of sectarian exclusivity, of moral self-righteousness, and so forth, we also must be mindful of a very important truth about life that was conveyed to us by Jack Fortin: *We are at our best when we speak from our center, not from our boundaries*—and we tend to compromise our lives when we lose sight of this center in our day-to-day lives.

In our pluralistic culture, we have tended to believe that the best approach to public conversations is to speak from the lowest common denominator. There is no doubt a place for this, but such an approach rarely enables the person to understand his or her deepest beliefs and the needed virtues to live out these beliefs. The lowest common denominator approach will disable the Christian from seeing the deep wisdom of the Gospels and the Christian tradition as it relates to work in general and entrepreneurship and business more specifically. They will shortchange their vocation and compromise the virtues necessary to live out their vocation. This disconnectedness between work and faith generates a practical atheism in the world today where one creates companies as if God did not exist, as if faith did not matter, as if there were no implications to one's work as it relates to eternal life.

All well and fine you may say, but what entrepreneurs actually think this way? What is often not told in the history of entrepreneurship and business is how many companies started with a vision that was informed by the religious faith of their founders, companies like Cadbury (Quaker), Herman Miller (Calvinist), Service Master (Evangelical), Dayton Hudson (Presbyterian), Cummings Engine (Disciples of Christ), Reell Precision Manufacturing (Lutheran/Covenant), Mondragon and Quimet-Cordon Bleu Foods Inc. (Catholic), and many others. We will explore several of these enterprises in this book, specifically how they have created faithful companies through practices, policies and critical decisions grounded within a Christian vision.

Christianity has developed a social tradition that *reconnects* the entrepreneur's work to a moral and spiritual vision of the enterprise—a reconnection of:

- work to the development of the worker
- ownership to the common good
- creation of goods and services to genuine needs
- distribution of wealth to the needs and merits of those who contribute
- organizational life to a community of work

This book seeks to reconnect for entrepreneurs the claims of their faith with the relationships and practices of their businesses. When Christian culture is at its best, it generates an economic order that humanizes the business realm in a way that generates faithful companies that enable them to see things whole, and not merely some of the parts.

Our point is not to say that the Christian religion is the only available source of humanizing our new entrepreneurial economy. Christianity does not have a monopoly on good work. But Christians and their institutions, particularly its churches and schools, have to face the seriousness of this new entrepreneurial reality if they are to be a light to the world. Christians as well as all religious believers must speak from their center *in such a way that allows others to do the same.* They have to respect and protect the religious liberty of others. They cannot proselytize by imposing their center on others, but they cannot at the same time evacuate their own religious core in the name of tolerance, diversity and pluralism. We believe that the focus on the virtues in the context of one's vocation provides the language and reality to achieve these goals simultaneously. The cultures we create in our entrepreneurial ventures in today's entrepreneurial economy will help shape the culture that our children and their children will share for years to come.

This is why we also believe that while we speak specifically from the Christian tradition, the virtues discussed in this book invite and encourage a deeper dialogue with other religious and cultural traditions to see the importance of integrating faith and business. This moral and spiritual level of engagement between faith and work will foster among religions deeper relations that prepare them to deal with the more difficult doctrinal differences they may have. But again, we will not learn great things from each other if we merely obey government laws and regulations or imitate the best practices of financial and operational techniques. These laws and markets are simply too small for the entrepreneurial soul. To feed and develop this soulfulness of the entrepreneur, we need to explore the two Vs—vocation and virtue.

Notes

1. David Brooks, "The Organization Kid," *The Atlantic Monthly* (April 2001): 40.
2. Ibid., p. 53.
3. See Bo Burlingham, Small Giants (New York: Portfolio, 2005).
4. "Research and Statistics," U.S. Small Business Association Office of Advocacy. http://www.sba.gov/advo/research/ (accessed July 2007).
5. When using examples from Jeff's experience, they will be told in the first person.

2

The Two *Vs*

The house of my soul is too small for you to come to it.
May it be enlarged by you.
St. Augustine

No man, for any period, can wear one face to himself and another to the
multitude without finally getting bewildered as to which may be true.
Nathanial Hawthorne

Before we get to the two *Vs* of vocation and virtue, we have to
deal with a problem that we touched on in our last chapter. It is
the problem of the divided life, the split between our faith and
our work. An analogy will help us see the problem. In London's
subway system, the traveler encounters both signs and a recording that warn her to "mind the gap" between the platform and
the train. This physical reality serves as a metaphor for what we
mean by the divided life, the gap between what we believe and
how we work. Yet, the principal problem is not the gap in our
lives, but in not recognizing the gap. When the traveler fails to
recognize the gap, she is in danger of tripping and falling.

One entrepreneur we know displays this recognition problem. He was reflecting to us on his career first as the entrepreneurial founder and subsequently CEO of the large public

company that his entrepreneurial efforts had produced. He remembered how on several different occasions his business had been on the verge of complete failure, and as soon as he resolved one crisis, another was not far behind. Although he had persevered and now had a business that had created incredible wealth both for his shareholders and for his family, he lamented the amount of time the business still seemed to require of him. Long hours and endless travel that took him away from his family was his lot in life. We asked him why he kept pushing so hard now that the business was so successful? Why had he sacrificed so much time from his family? After all, his net worth was estimated to be over $100 million. "Because I want to be worth $200 million" was his reply.

This entrepreneur considers himself to be a good Christian who goes to church every Sunday and contributes to local charities, but he seemed to have little awareness of the gap between his desire to be *worth more* and *to be more*. He seemed to have little capacity to do an honest gap analysis between the gospel warnings on wealth and his rather crass desire for more. As his business was increasingly taking up more time, energy and thought, he had little recognition that his business was becoming the predominant and overwhelming force in his life. The danger for the entrepreneur is not so much the gap itself but the failure to recognize that there is a gap to be minded.

Yet this gap and its recognition failure are also found within us in subtle ways. While most of us would never say that making money or having status and fame are the only important goals in life, we find ourselves falling into patterns as if they were. We usually will not verbally articulate these values, but if we analyze the emotional tapes in our heads that have been playing for years, we may be shocked at what we really value. We find ourselves too often compromising human relationships for business opportunities, status symbols and higher standards of living. Our particular compromises are not usually earth shattering at the moment they are made, but we too frequently fall into patterns that opt for work (careerism) or consumption (consumerism) over God, spouses, children and community. Our compromises over a lifetime come to full effect near the end of our lives as we discover that we have thin relationships with God, family and community.

This split between faith and work, between business and religious life is a symptom of a much larger problem of our human condition—original sin. St. Paul and St. Augustine were profoundly conscious of this division—it is precisely one element of their sainthood. In the New Testament, Paul writes, "What I do I do not understand. For I do not do what I want, but I do what I hate. . . . The willing is ready at hand, but doing the good is not. For I do not do the good I want, but I do the evil I do not want" (Rom. 7:15,18-19). Augustine calls this internal conflict and division the "monstrous fact." In the *Confessions*, he explained his own suffering from what he describes as two wills that were divided from each other, neither of which was complete, and what was present in the one will was lacking in the other.

Yet, while this divided life is part of our fallen nature, there is something about our modern age, and increasingly our culture, that has made this division even more difficult to recognize. Whereas in the past our culture would challenge such a split with claims of hypocrisy, duplicity and sin, today our culture has created a language that has normalized not just distinctions but separations or walls between public/private, faith/work, body/soul, church/state, spirituality/religion, reason/revelation, and so forth. These divisions have so compartmentalized the deepest sources of meaning of our lives from the most significant actions in how we live and work, that this split has come to be seen as a normal state of affairs. Our culture not only fails to challenge this compartmentalization, but it also works particularly hard at avoiding its confrontation by denying the fact that we are divided.

Our culture also has influenced the way we understand entrepreneurship, which fosters rifts within the entrepreneur. Wanting something more from their work, some people become entrepreneurs by leaving large corporations (or to avoid ever having to work in them) to start new companies that can be better places to work, where they can be freer to exercise their own ethics and values, and create stronger communities of work. Certainly part of what motivates these entrepreneurs is the potential to make a profit though technical improvements of a product and service; that is, they want to make something better or provide better service to the customer. But, beyond improving business practices, many entrepreneurs yearn to create places that are better to work in, that treat employees more fairly and with more respect for their contributions.

For example, when my partners and I (Jeff) made the decision to start our health-care company, we deliberately sought to treat our employees differently from the norm in the industry. A common practice at that time was to use frequent lay-offs to adjust to the normal fluctuations in demand for services that would push census in facilities up and down from week to week. We decided that we wanted to make sure that our employees would not suffer from such economic instability just to assure the maximization of our profits. We had seen how these common employment practices hurt morale in the industry and caused hardships for many dedicated health-care professionals.

However, the original commitment to create a better place to work can get challenged by the day-to-day reality of keeping a business on stable financial ground. The financial and productive troubles and pressures in starting and running a business can cause the entrepreneur to shift the focus simply for the survival of the business. It is often at this point where an entrepreneurial venture begins to start to look like the company we left, as was seen in Jeff's example from the previous chapter.

One reason that so many entrepreneurs slide back to "business as usual," creating in the entrepreneur a divide between the moral insights of faith and the practices and policies of the company, stems from their education and formation. Too often their education about entrepreneurship focuses only on the technical realm of the new venture process, leaving them unprepared to create a unique moral culture that is different from the typical business model. Opportunity assessment, resource acquisition, feasibility analysis, business planning, financing, and managing growth are all critical technical skills that an entrepreneur needs to understand or even master to be effective. These techniques and skills are paramount to the economic survival of a business venture. Yet reducing entrepreneurial success solely to technical and financial measurements is a serious problem in the business world. In doing so, we reduce human work to simply a factor of production to be used to maximize financial performance and growth. Most entrepreneurs seek more than this from the risks they take to launch their new ventures.

To reduce our gaps and divisions, we have to look at the *whole* of our lives. And the place we find the whole is the place we find God helping us live the life we were intended to live, and this is the meaning of our vocation. And what enables us to live out this vocation are the virtues—those good habits that pattern our lives not only occasionally but also daily in the pressures, complexities, difficulties and opportunities of business. It is this sense of vocation and virtues that helps us constantly reorder the situations we face toward the good of others, ourselves and God.

The Vocation of the Good Entrepreneur: An Ordering of Goods

I like Earl Nightingale's description of success: "Success is the progressive realization of a worthy idea." This definition helps us understand that success is not an end goal; a place you reach; something you have. Instead, success is a journey, an evolution, a point on a continuum of life. Therefore, this company we're building is successful. We have a worthy idea and we're executing it in ways that we believe are pleasing to God.

Clyde Lear, CEO and Founder, Learfield Communication

The divide that is experienced by many entrepreneurs is at its core a spiritual and moral disorder. The remedy to this divide, to this moral and spiritual disease, is the discernment of one's vocation, a way to order life. The Christian tradition speaks about vocation in terms of three callings: a calling to be human, a calling to belong to community, and a calling to a way of doing work. There are of course other ways to speak of one's vocation, but for entrepreneurs, we have found that this approach helps them to order the various parts of their lives into a more cohesive whole. Bill Lee, president and CEO of Lee Company, explained to us that a vocation "is having the sense that I am fulfilling that which I have been called to do. And to the degree that I feel I am fulfilling that, then, I am being successful. So in order to be successful, you have to have an understanding of what you are really called to be." Without this sense of call, one's definition of success tends to be superficially defined, usually by monetary value or by organizational titles.

A Calling to Be Human

One of the first things the Christian tradition challenges the entrepreneur on is his temptation to think of himself only as an entrepreneur. The first vocation for the entrepreneur in the Christian tradition is not only to be an entrepreneur but also to be *fully human*, to be who he was created to be. The question for us is not what I want to be, but what I *need* to be. God calls us out of nothing and chaos into being, to be an image of God, destined for His kingdom and to love in the here and now.

This call to be human, to be who we were meant to be, is difficult for us, since we are always tempted to equate our achievements in work with our identity of who we are. The first question we, as Americans, often ask people in conversations is, "What do you do?" Our response is most often to define who we are in terms of what work we do. "I'm an entrepreneur." "I'm a manager." "I am a teacher." "I'm a doctor." These are all nouns that define our humanness in the single dimension of our work. There is no doubt that people's achievements are connected to their character, but we need to resist becoming the noun of what we do for a living. We are more than our work suggests. While God has called each of us in a unique way through our own inclinations, interests, aptitudes and predilections, God has created us not only to work, but also to rest—to rest in worship, contemplation, family, community and nature.

We seem to create folk heroes out of entrepreneurs who expend Herculean efforts to achieve success in their businesses. And while this is good to a point, if entrepreneurial success comes at the expense of our marriage, our families, our faith and our friendships, it is a hollow victory. If all we have at the end of our lives is our wealth—if that is all we leave behind— that is not a life well lived. As the old saying goes, *You never see a hearse with a luggage rack.*

Entrepreneurs often fall into the temptation to interpret their vocation in terms of only what they do, and in particular, what they do successfully. This can be very tragic, since there is a good chance their ventures will fall into crisis some day: the loss of a major customer, key people quit, insurmountable problems with a partner, drastic and sudden changes in the market that cannot be addressed, serious illness—all leading to bankruptcy. If then, while in crisis, they have no resources of who they are besides entrepreneurs, they will be in total crisis. But if in such a crisis they can fall back on a more expansive notion of a deeper identity that goes beyond their work, their crisis can be a real opportunity for significant personal growth.

In the 1970s, when my (Mike's) dad, Noel Naughton, decided to make the leap in his construction business (Woodman Construction) from building single houses to building several houses at one time, he could not predict the significant spike in mortgage interest rates and rising construction costs that were about to occur. When Noel finished building the houses, mortgage interest rates were close to an all-time high of 20 percent, and construction costs rose faster than inflation. Combined with a poor pricing model that undersold the houses, the losses were close to $250,000.

While my dad never went into bankruptcy or drew on unemployment, the frustration and the pain of losing so much money and working 16-hour days with no equity to show for it took a toll on him. The worries and anxiety made him physically ill. He also started to drink more. He became more moody and more distant from his kids. Yet his economic crisis as an entrepreneur also became a spiritual opportunity. His valley, and it was a dark valley, became a time for real spiritual fruit to grow. Abraham Lincoln once said, "I have been driven many times to my knees by the overwhelming conviction that I had nowhere else to go." My dad had nowhere else to go, and with the help of his wife, his church and some very good friends, he found himself more humbled, more open to the Scriptures, more prone to pray.

This spiritual perspective did not take away the worries and pain, but it did help him see that his identity was not Woodman Construction—that no matter how difficult life is, God can redeem us in our failures. It was also at this time that Mother

Teresa's saying became very real to him: *God wants us first to be faithful, not successful.* Of course, it would be nice to be both, but that was not in the cards this time around.

A Calling to Belong to Community

The second calling of one's vocation relates to the broader context of where the entrepreneur lives out this vocation. For many of us, it is lived out in marriage. So we speak of our vocation as a wife, a husband, a mother, a father that is prior to one's vocation as an entrepreneur. The community that we call family is what many of us call the primary community that has certain claims on us. As a wise colleague of ours, Bob Kennedy, put it, "My wife has only one husband. My children have only one father." Or as Paul Orfalea, founder of Kinko's, explained, "Success in life is having kids who want to come back to visit you when they've grown up." Family life cannot be sacrificed to an entrepreneurial enterprise. Period!

Yet the entrepreneur cannot escape the tensions between family and work. Starting and building a business can take up much more time and much more energy than is often expected. No one puts boundaries on this effort except for the entrepreneur himself. There is no boss to set work objectives or to tell us to take a day off. Therefore, one of the biggest challenges for an entrepreneur is the tension between work and family. It requires an intentionality of actions and decisions to manage this tension with any success (see chapter 6 for suggestions to manage this tension).

For entrepreneurs engaged in family businesses, the tension between business and family often becomes more pronounced. One would assume that since they engage in the business together, operating a family business would alleviate some of the conflicting demands for time and energy from the entrepreneur. But in many ways, a family business can make the calling to community more complex. Family issues and business issues blur together, preventing either from being fully or even adequately addressed. While no family can achieve this goal in an absolute sense, family business should continuously strive to minimize the mix of family and business.

For example, a married couple we know, Steve and Carolyn, run their family consulting business out of their home. They learned that to create more separation between family and business, they needed to each set up their own office in the home—they called them their north and south offices. Once work was done, they made a point of closing the doors to their offices and not going back in until the next day's work began.

The community that is our family and the community that is our work have very different needs that each requires attention. Simply bringing our family into our business does not assure that our calling as a husband, a wife, a mother or a father is given its due. Even in a family business it is essential to view our families and our businesses as distinct communities and create times and events that give the business a rest.

A Calling to a Way of Working: Exercising Our Gifts

Yet, even though work does not exhaust this vocation to our humanity, and our work should not supersede our families, work is a very important dimension of our vocation precisely because we feel called to a particular kind of way of working. When speaking to entrepreneurs, they will often describe their experience of starting the business as being *called*. Now, this call is expressed through a wide variety of reasons. For some, it is about the money, although we have found this not as common as most people think. For others, and we have found this more often to be the case, they believe that it is work that fits their personality. They feel that the independence and autonomy that entrepreneurship offers fit them. They want to be their own boss. They don't want people telling them what to do all day. They want to see the implications of a vision they have in their mind. They feel compelled to be leaders and in control. They derive pleasure out of the process of creating and building something out of nothing. It is a style of work that they feel called to do and fits with what gives them strong satisfaction from their efforts.

For Jim Stefansic, the cofounder of a medical device company we will explore in greater detail in chapter 6, starting his venture allowed him to not only pursue his talents as an engineer and scientist but also to apply his business skills. He says that he is more fulfilled and satisfied than he has ever been, even though the stress of a start-up is more than he could have imagined.

We can also see this path to entrepreneurship in Alexis, the self-employed artist who has found commercial outlets for her art in studios and by creating commissioned work, or in Steve, the physician who established a private practice to exercise his gift of healing. Engineers, musicians, architects, physical therapists, writers, and so on, all can find an entrepreneurial vocation in their specific area of interest and training.

We have found, however, that if the call to start a business does not go deeper than money, autonomy and even creating a particular product, something begins to go wrong in the enterprise. An analogy to marriage can be helpful here. People go into marriage for all sorts of reasons—physical attraction, alleviation of loneliness, emotional elation, personal compatibility—but what often attracted couples to get married is not enough to keep them in a good marriage. While there are many attributes of a good marriage, a central element to marriage is self-gift—the capacity to give to and serve the other for the common good.

In a similar way, if entrepreneurs do not move beyond their own interests in describing the success of their business, they are headed for a bad business. The entrepreneur has to define the success of his business beyond financial, technical and market achievements to moral and spiritual principles that reveal the business as a gift to others. This may initially sound a bit too moralistic and idealistic. We have found, however, that when entrepreneurs describe their success and satisfaction with their company in broader criteria than merely financial gain, they are on the way to setting a foundation on which to build a company that is faithful to their deeper commitments. Some of the criteria include:

- creating jobs in which employees can find security
- generating and distributing wealth for their investors and their employees
- developing a highly positive culture that attracts workers who see the business as a good place to work
- maintaining low rates of employee turnover and high employee satisfaction
- providing needed services and products with great quality

No matter what path leads us to become entrepreneurs, the only way we can be fully human in our work is if we see our work as an opportunity to give our talents to others in service to the good of society and to God. Martin Luther put this point in very concrete terms when he wrote that if a person is a Christian tailor, for example, he will say the following: "I make these clothes because God has bidden me to do so, so that I can earn a living, so that I can help and serve my neighbor. When a Christian does not serve the other, God is not present; that is not Christian living."

So when we speak of our vocation to work, we are speaking about how we use our gifts to serve others and bring forth God's presence in the world. We are at our best not when we are taking, or calculating our interests, or maximizing our utilities, or shouting claims of freedom, but when we give of ourselves for social and spiritual purposes. This vocation to be human is a call that is heard by the sheer fact that we are created, which makes it a universal call. All people are called to give themselves in the work they do, whether one is an entrepreneur, a tailor, a manager or a plumber. This call, this voice of creation, reveals to us that a core dimension of our identity is found in giving ourselves to others and to God in the work we do. This is not a reality we can deny, unless we want to deny ourselves. This dynamic of self-gift is a natural law of sorts—if we break it, we break ourselves.

One of the more powerful stories that illuminate this understanding of gift in our lives is found in Lewis Hyde's book *The Gift*, where he speaks of the "gift economy." Hyde explains that when Native Americans encountered Puritans in their first set of gift encounters, they were baffled by their possessiveness over gifts given them. Native Americans expected their English visitors to give back their gifts in order to keep them moving. This idea of setting gifts in motion equally baffled the Europeans, who negatively characterized Native Americans as "Indian givers."[1]

Yet, what Native Americans understood, and what we should take heed of, is that when a gift is not shared, it corrupts the holder. The one who makes the gift an occasion for selfish hoarding, who fails to put the gift in motion in service to others, becomes corrupted by the gift itself. So the moral and spiritual core of an entrepreneurial business is not greed, but gifts; not with taking, but with giving; not with self-interest, but with the other's good.

The Virtues: The Habits of a Good Entrepreneur

If our work is to be a vocation, a form of giving, we need to see our work in terms of the virtues—good habits that connect us with others while building strong character within us. It is the virtues that give our vocation legs and arms by developing within us habits that help us respond with goodness in all that we do. The virtues take our vocation from aspiration to realization in the habits and patterns of our life as well as the specific policies and procedures of how we organize our work.

When we speak of virtue, we are describing not merely an abstract theory of morality, but how people actually behave and what happens to them in their behavior. At root, an understanding of the virtues makes explicit for us something obvious: When we choose good habits, we become good; we build character to act rightly in tough situations. From a more specifically Christian view, the obvious insight is that the virtues are those good habits that enable us to be the person God has created us to be. Vices, on the contrary, are those bad habits that fail to build character and that prevent us from becoming the person God has created us to be. When we steal on a habitual basis, we become thieves, which are not the kind of people we were made to be.

A central understanding of virtue hinges on the observation that our character is formed not simply by the large decisions that alter the course of our life, but also by the small daily decisions we make about particular matters in our family, work and community involvement. Our moral growth takes place in the patterns and habits of response in the daily encounters of our life. Virtues are the name we give to those habitual patterns that bring out those goods that lie within us to which we are *called*.

Critical to understanding the importance of virtue for the entrepreneur, then, is to see the impact virtues have on his or her character. The work of an entrepreneur, or any worker, is not only about achieving objectives. The entrepreneur changes not only the world, but he also changes himself. He not only makes a choice about what to make, but he also makes a choice about what type of person he becomes. Work not only goes out of the person and changes things, but like a mirror, it reflects right back into the person.

This reflection of work on the character of the person is often seen more clearly in retirement. Many entrepreneurs and business people have a hard time retiring from their businesses because the habits they formed have been too often restricted to the narrow financial and productive goals of the organization and their own careerist aspirations. For example, two years after Lee Iacocca retired, his picture was on the cover of *Fortune* magazine with the line "How I flunked retirement." Lee Iacocca, this icon of American industry, this economic giant, this man who knew exactly who he was as chairman of the Chrysler Corporation, was uneasy, unsure and somewhat lost in retirement. While he developed habits of work, he seemingly neglected other virtues important to his personhood. As John Ruskin put it, "The highest reward [or punishment] for one's work is not what he gets from it, but what he becomes by it." Lee Iacocca's work generated great wealth and impressive titles, but something was neglected in contributing to his whole person. Of course, one of the impressive things about Iacocca is that he had the guts and honesty to reflect in public about this issue.

When a person works, he affects the inner landscape of his character. The issue is not whether he changes himself, but how he changes himself. And the key to understanding the significant revealing of his personhood is not found in the amount of revenues he has generated, or levels of promotions, or the percentage of market share he has captured. Rather, the moral and spiritual character of an entrepreneur or businessperson will be captured in the responsible relationships he has forged with others in the actions of running his business. More specifically, this can be shaped by the opportunities he pursues, who he chooses to do business with, who he hires, decisions he makes about products and markets, decisions about whether and how fast to grow, the corporate culture he builds, and his engagement with the community as a leader and/or citizen. At the heart of these relationships are the virtues, which we will explore in the next four chapters.

This change in the person does not come all at once, but gradually. It is often imperceptible in individual acts, but eventually one begins to see a pattern of activity or habits that leave deeper and deeper impressions, forming what we often call the character of the person. If these habits are good, we call them virtues and they develop our character. If the habits are bad, we call them vices and they cause our character to become disordered.

The purpose of a business is never *only* to make money, or to produce a product or service, but to accomplish these goals in such a manner that the entrepreneur and those he works with become better people. It is precisely in the development of people that the dignity of the entrepreneur is derived.

Of course the entrepreneur who fails to make money is no longer an entrepreneur; he is broke. But his work is never fully, or essentially, explained by the money he makes or the products and services he provides. In other words, to explain the work of the entrepreneur by his profits or product is to remain on a superficial surface of what is actually happening. Yet, one of the things that most entrepreneurs will tell you is that they have little time to think or even be aware of the changes to their character through their work. Thus, they ignore one of the most enduring questions for the entrepreneur: *What kind of entrepreneur should I become?*

None of this is meant to escape or alleviate the technical difficulties and financial pressures of starting and growing a business. If entrepreneurs were to create organizations without due regard to the performance of their business, chaos would reign as a prelude to failure. But in a similar way, if they were to create ventures without recognizing the importance of striving to become good in what they do and how they do it, chaos of a different order would reign, namely, the moral and spiritual stagnation of the entrepreneurs who create these businesses.

What the virtues help us name is the kinds of habits and patterns that are necessary for the entrepreneur and her business to become good. The Christian and Western tradition has a lot to say about virtues, which we will explore in more detail in the next four chapters. We will focus on the traditional four cardinal virtues. The reason we focus on these four virtues is that we believe that entrepreneurs cannot live their vocation without them. We also believe that a business cannot make moral sense without them.

Everyone will agree that the virtues of industriousness, as well as ingenuity, diligence, frugality, and so forth, are necessary for an entrepreneur to be successful. But what the Christian tradition points out is that these virtues are insufficient in what comprises the *good entrepreneur*, since they fail to activate and order the *giving* dimension of her vocation. These so-called entrepreneurial virtues can only be moral and spiritual virtues if they *make us more human*, and they can only make us more human if we are ultimately helping other people to develop.

Here we come to one of the most important insights of the Christian tradition on work and its relationship to virtue: *We grow as human beings at work to the extent that we create conditions for other people to develop.* In other words, we cannot develop ourselves at work without developing others at work, and we cannot develop others unless we ourselves are trying to be virtuous. When our goal in work disengages from the moral and spiritual order in which it is done (the vocational order), a certain corruption occurs within us. When our goal is simply to win a league championship, we are prone to lose our sportsmanship; when our goal is merely to raise an audience's laughter, we can slip into vulgarity; and when our goal is solely to maximize wealth, we are inclined to use people to achieve that end and become like *entrepreneurs on steroids*—those who pursue the maximization of wealth no matter what the cost to our employees and families.

The virtues of prudence, justice, courage and temperance are not simply four arbitrary habits that someone thought of on the fly; they are four characteristics that have been thought about for more than 3,000 years. They have been developed by Jewish, Muslim, Catholic and Protestant thinkers, and examined by philosophers such as Aristotle and Confucius.

The reason why we think these virtues are such a powerful way to think about being an entrepreneur is that they reveal how we actually operate. What do we mean here? When an entrepreneur works, she uses her head, her will and her heart. The Christian tradition has identified four such dispositions, calling them *cardinal* virtues, from the Latin for "hinge." To do well "hinges" on these four virtues in the sense that no matter what end we are seeking or what means we employ, if we are to do *well,* we must perform every action prudently, justly, courageously and temperately. These four cardinal virtues are primary because they reveal to us how we act when we are at our best.

So who is the *good entrepreneur*?

• The good entrepreneur is intelligent and technically competent. She is a good steward of the resources and gifts she has available. She is prudent.

• The good entrepreneur builds strong relationships in her family, with employees in her business and in the broader society. She does this by being just.

• The good entrepreneur overcomes obstacles in building her company, but does so without ever compromising what she knows to be truly right. She does this with courage.

• The good entrepreneur moderates her work ethic with rest. She does this through temperance.

The next four chapters will explore each of these four virtues as they play out in the start-up and growth of an entrepreneurial venture. Each chapter will offer stories and practical techniques that can help an entrepreneur bring these virtues to life in business. Taken together, these chapters can provide a road map of what a vocation to entrepreneurship and business looks like in the day-to-day operations of real organizations.

Note
1. Lewis Hyde, *The Gift: Imagination and the Erotic Life of Property* (New York: Random House, 1983), pp. 3-4.

PART TWO

The Four Cardinal Virtues

3

Prudence:
Being Wise Stewards

*Only those who combine an ethics of calculation with an ethics of
conviction can truly experience [their role and function] as a vocation.*
PAUL RICOEUR

When Joe Keeley started his company, College Nannies and
Tutors Development, Inc., he wrestled with his role as that of a
steward of the resources he was managing. On one hand he saw
other entrepreneurs getting outside investment funding and
then turning around to pay themselves generous salaries. They
would rationalize such salaries by the hours they worked, the
risks they took, the talents they brought to the enterprise. Such
entrepreneurs often characterized their business as a game, and
their role was to be clever in winning the game. The smart entrepreneur was one who calculated his own interests in a sea of
other conflicting claims and always made sure that his interests
came out on top.

This small-minded mentality of self-preservation was not
the way that Joe wanted to run his business. Such a view of entrepreneurship repelled him. But Joe is struggling with an oppo-
site problem. "While I very much try to keep what I take out of

the business as minimal as possible, I have become frustrated by an entry-level salary that has not kept up with my cost of living. I now have a daughter, so my family responsibilities are in tension with my business responsibilities. I still want to keep pouring any extra money back into the business, rather than increasing my salary. And I think that's what my investors also expect. But I also have to think of my family."

I (Jeff) remember vividly my own experience. It was the day that an investor put money into our business. When it came time to close his investment, I was somewhat surprised when the investor took out his personal checkbook. It was an ordinary looking checkbook with a vinyl cover. I had envisioned a more formal transaction, with a business check or even a wire transfer. But, it was the same checkbook that he used to pay his monthly personal bills. The check had his home address. It was a typical looking check with a farm scene in the background. There was an old wooden fence with a bird perched on the post. At the moment I looked at the check, I was struck by the fact that this person was about to make a very large investment in our business using his own personal funds—written from a check from his personal checking account! The whole scene brought home to me the responsibility we faced to take good care of this investor's money.

Too often entrepreneurs are cast as cunning and opportunistic, tacticians who conceal their real intentions to deceive others in order to achieve their own self-centered goals. While there are certainly entrepreneurs who fall within this Machiavellian mindset, it does not describe the motivations of most entrepreneurs. Joe Keeley and others like him are less like those who calculate their own self-interest and more like stewards of the common good. While they want to receive a good salary from their business, as well as equity, the resources they deploy as entrepreneurs are not theirs alone.

Yet, like Joe Keeley, they struggle with the practical problems of what is fair and effective in particular situations. As they secure the necessary resources from a variety of sources—financing from investors or bankers, labor from employees, materials from suppliers, contracts from customers, space from landlords, time away from their family; they wrestle with the practical dimensions of managing these relationships. As stewards of these resources, they are expected to use them productively in such a way that a return is given to each of the stakeholders. The challenge of the entrepreneur is how to contribute resources to certain people while not taking from others.

The virtue of prudence helps the entrepreneur make decisions that effectively allow her and the organization to be wise stewards for all her stakeholders. The prudent entrepreneur is a person who has the necessary entrepreneurial skills, perceives the situation as it is and directs her activity toward good ends that multiply the resources of the world. She is not one who draws from the resources of the world, but is a contributor.

In this chapter, we will provide a general description of the prudent entrepreneur as understood within the Christian tradition. We will particularly focus on how prudence connects and synthesizes effective means to good ends in the right circumstances. We will also discuss the counterfeits of prudence, since the ordinary use of the term too often confuses what has been traditionally meant by it.

A Primer on Prudence:
Integrating Means and Ends

Prudence is concerned not only with what is right, but also that what is done is done rightly; not only with what is good, but that it is done well. Entrepreneurial prudence has three components:

- the careful stewardship of the resources available to the entrepreneur
- the pursuit of morally good ends
- the particular and unique circumstances faced by each entrepreneur in each new venture

In other words, recognizing the responsibility to use the resources made available by various stakeholders of the business, the entrepreneur has to discern the most effective *means* for attaining the firm's morally good *ends* in light of his particular and unique *circumstances*.

Means: The Art of Entrepreneurial Skills

Each of us, made in the image of God, has been given a command to have dominion, to "make" something (see Gen. 1:26). Entrepreneurs in particular are by nature builders and makers of things. To start and grow a business, the entrepreneur develops the necessary business skills needed to transform the resources secured by various stakeholders—raw materials, labor, money, and so forth—into useful products and services.

For example, Joe Keeley developed systems and processes, which are his techniques, to transform software systems, the skills of his nannies, the capital from his investors, the investments from his franchisees, and so forth, into a business that helps connect skilled nannies with families seeking trustworthy help in caring for their children. The mastery of such skills and means are what makes it possible for an entrepreneur to build an enterprise. If the best means are not used, then the entrepreneur is placing the enterprise at a risk of failure that is irresponsible.

This desire to make things, to be creative, is a response to a very obvious truth of the created order: things are not ready-made in nature, but rather they need our work to bring out their usefulness. This process of making is one of transforming the entrepreneur's creative ideas into marketable and useful products and services through viable and sustainable business ventures. It is the recognition and pursuit of market opportunities and the securing of the resources necessary to successfully launch and grow a new venture. Through a collection of techniques and skills, the entrepreneur deciphers, calculates, interprets, strategizes and perceives what is necessary to achieve particular goals.

Bootstrapping is one such technique, which we will examine later in this chapter. It is a process of finding creative ways to launch and grow businesses with the limited resources available for most start-up ventures. Bootstrapping includes techniques and tactics needed to keep a business operating, which cover all of the functions of running a business—from marketing, to staffing, to inventory and production management, to cash flow management, to the administrative processes. Bootstrapping helps entrepreneurs reach their goals for their businesses in the face of very limited resources. Beyond just finding ways to start a business when resources are limited, bootstrapping a venture can make it financially stronger. By creating a business that is more efficient with its available resources, the entrepreneur requires less outside funding, enabling him to control the direction of the company. Making a virtue of necessity, bootstrapping can enable the entrepreneur to be a careful steward of the limited resources he has available to start and grow the business.

Good Ends: The Nobility of Entrepreneurship

However important the means are to entrepreneurship, and they are very important, they have to be directed not simply to any old end, but to *good ends* if the entrepreneur is to develop the enterprise into a community of work where people flourish. Our call to have dominion over the earth does not mean exploitation or domination, but a way in which we do our work. The book of Genesis tells us that God's creation is not only a one-time event but also an unfolding process in which we have been asked to participate in God's command to us to have dominion through the work we do. The constant question for all of us is whether we participate in this call to collaborate with God or frustrate God's created order through our self-interested order. Human work can express a sharing in the divine work of creation or it can express a violation of the created order, depending on the ends that are chosen. By putting to use the wealth of spiritual and material resources given to us by God, we can contribute to the progress of society and our own development by allowing all people to participate in this dominion.

This vocational understanding of the *ends* is why the *means* of entrepreneurship is never enough for the entrepreneur. Bootstrapping, for example, is indifferent to whether it is producing tobacco or life-saving devices. The Web communicates vice and virtue alike. The prudent entrepreneur has to understand the end for which she is working just as much as she understands the means she is using.

What does it mean for the entrepreneur to have a good end? This question is a profoundly moral and spiritual question because it entails an ongoing reflection not only upon our intentions, our desires, our dreams and our relationships, but even more importantly, the purification of our intentions, desires, dreams and relationships.

This purification of our end is greatly determined by the culture in which the entrepreneur has been formed, as we discussed in chapter 1. The end of an entrepreneur's work will depend greatly on his family of origin, his friends, his schooling, his principles, his religious convictions, that is, the culture out of which he was formed. This formation is not a guarantee of virtue or vice, but it will predispose the entrepreneur to act in one way or another. If we have not been cultured in an environment in which we have moral witnesses, noble stories and spiritual principles, but instead where our individual preferences are primary, our consumptive wants prevail and our careerist aspirations dominate, the chances of intending good ends will be difficult.

One witness to the power of ends is the story of Oskar Schindler, a German entrepreneur whose enterprise was used to save close to 1,000 Jews from German concentration camps. His story is retold in the movie *Schindler's List*. At the beginning of his enterprise, however, Schindler had little interest in saving

Jews or, for that matter, promoting the Nazi cause. As he tells his wife at the beginning of his enterprise, "I have 350 [Jewish] workers on the factory floor with one purpose: to make money— for me!" For Schindler the entrepreneur, the Jews and the Nazis were both used as instruments toward his end of profit.

Gradually, however, his eyes were opened to the brutality of the Nazi project, and his end of profit maximization increasingly took on a hollowness of meaning. He also became nervously aware of a chilling revelation: He was becoming more like the Nazis than he thought. While he prided himself on his neutrality toward the Nazi cause, his use of the Jewish workers for his own profit was simply another form of exploitation and domination, but cloaked in the form of a company rather than a national ideology. His seeming morally neutral economic position of profit maximization could no longer be sustained.

What enabled Schindler to see the injustice done to the Jews and do something about it in his work is difficult to determine precisely, but his mother's religious guidance, his boyhood Jewish friends, his strong-willed father as well as other cultural contributions helped him see what his work was doing to him.

When an entrepreneur thinks about the end or purpose for which he starts the enterprise, he needs to discern interiorly what kind of person he is becoming and whether his work is moving him toward his calling in life, how it is impacting his family, the effect the product or service is having on the customer, and whether he is fostering a community of work for the employees and investors who are connected with the enterprise. The grounding of these *relationships* is informed by the moral virtues of justice, courage and temperance, which for most people are developed in the cultural institutions of family, religion and school. The desire for the end that these virtues promote will come through a vibrant culture, which fosters an understanding that the entrepreneur's business is not his own private affair but an opportunity to exercise his gifts in service to others. What prudence enables the entrepreneur to do is determine and adjust the effective and proper means to attain and strengthen these right relationships.

We can visualize what it takes to be a prudent entrepreneur by examining the relationship between means and ends. Consider the following simple matrix:

Prudence and Its Counterfeits

	Ineffective Means	Effective Means
Good Ends	(2) Well intentioned (moralistic)	(4) Prudent (flourish)
Bad Ends	(1) Incompetent (broke)	(3) Cunning (survival)

1. Incompetent (Bad Ends/Ineffective Means)

There are the *incompetent,* those unfortunate souls who have neither good ends nor effective means. Sometimes, due mostly to good luck, even the incompetent entrepreneur can realize success. The nature of the opportunity is so wide open, so rich, that almost any entrant into the market can gain sales and market share. But their existence is usually short-lived. Soon those who employ effective means will begin to force the incompetent out of the market.

In the year 2000 the dot-com craze was rife with examples of incompetent entrepreneurs. One example was the ill-fated story of Pets.com. The business model was that all businesses were going to move to the Web. Bricks and mortar operations would soon be driven out of business by dot-com operations. For the founders of Pets.com, this included pet supplies. They planned to sell things like bags of dog food and kitty litter through the Web direct to customers' homes. There were fatal flaws in the model, however. First of all, the shipping costs were prohibitive. To be price competitive with grocery and pet stores, they had to sell the product at a price that did not cover the cost of the product and the shipping costs. They lost money on every item they sold. Also, it took several days to get the product to a customer's home. Customers usually buy these products as they run out—they cannot wait two to four days. In the end, even though the business model could never work, they raised more than $80 million. Like so many other dot-com businesses during that time, it was not about building a sustainable business. The goal was to raise a large sum of money, make a few people very rich and not worry about the fact that the business was doomed from the start.

2. Well-intentioned (Good Ends/Ineffective Means)

Well-intentioned entrepreneurs want to create a good product, help their employees grow and serve the community, but they do not have effective means to implement such good ends. For example, when organic food first became popular in the early 2000s, almost any supplier could sell product. The price and the quality of the food did not seem to matter; as long as it was labeled "organic" people would buy it. But as the market grew and attracted more farmers and more of the traditional food distributors, it was the competent competitors who began to attract the customers. Those who were incompetent, that is, those who did not produce quality food and get it efficiently to the market, went out of business. Customers recognized their incompetence and shifted their business to others who could effectively meet their needs.

We see this well-intentioned ineffectiveness with many social entrepreneurs who are trying desperately to address social issues by founding nonprofit entities. They have their heart in the right place, but they lack the necessary competency to fulfill the ends they want. Often they lack effective insights and practices in terms of finance, production and marketing on a *regular* basis. For example, in studies of charter school failures, it has been shown that administrative and financial management problems are by far the leading cause of collapse. While we call these entrepreneurs well intentioned, we should not call them virtuous in their work. They tend to display virtues such as justice, kindness and courage, but very imperfectly, because they cannot institutionalize the fullness of the virtue through sound productive means of finance, operations, marketing and overall good management. As we will discuss in the next three chapters, however, justice, courage and temperance are only virtues when they are united with prudence, and thus are imperfect for the well intentioned. In the words of one successful nonprofit executive: "We have no mission without an ability to create adequate margin."

3. Cunning (Bad Ends/Effective Means)
Despite the character and technical problems of the well intentioned and incompetent, these two characters will be out of

business sooner rather than later. But the most enduring counterfeit of prudence resides in those who confuse being prudent with being *cunning*. They can be highly efficient, technically competent and have a great sense of timing, but their purpose is only for themselves. To have technical skill without good ends can unleash a powerfully destructive force in society.

George Soros, a financial speculator, for example, made a billion dollars speculating against the British pound, leaving the British economy severely damaged. He viewed his financial techniques in morally neutral terms. He was aware of negative effects of speculation: "I never think about them and cannot afford to think about them. If I stopped doing some things because of moral scruples, I would have to stop being a speculator. I feel no remorse whatsoever about having won money when the pound was devalued; I did not speculate against the pound to help England or hurt her; I did it to earn money."[1] Soros, as much as he may try, cannot separate his ruinous behavior on England from the kind of person he is becoming. Nor can he make up for it with contributions to charities. As Thomas Schaffer and Robert Rodes point out, "If you spend the day on corporate takeovers and plant closings without thinking about the people you put out of work, you cannot make up for the harm you do by giving a woman free legal advice in the evening when her unemployed husband takes out his frustration by beating her."[2]

It is important to realize that the cunning are not always vicious. The cunning often do good things, but for self-interested and utility-driven reasons. Entrepreneurs, in general, are not going to rip off customers, treat employees poorly, manipulate investors, and so forth The primary cause for what is cunning is not only the act that is done but the intention behind the end for which it is done. The problem with the intention of the cunning is that the appearance of virtue is argued as long as no great sacrifices are demanded. I will treat my employees well because such treatment maximizes productivity and efficiency. This is the shortcoming of much of the writings on corporate social responsibility. There are endless studies that try to link being socially responsible with improved financial performance.

But what happens when such good treatment entails heavy sacrifice? The cunning are suddenly thrown off, since their belief that "good treatment equals greater profits" is not working. This is why prudence is never prudence unless accompanied by justice, courage and temperance—those virtues that order our intentions and desires away from calculating self-interest, greed, envy, fear and all the other deadly vices that corrupt the soul. These virtues not only change our actions and transform our intentions, but they also prepare us to make sacrifices when needed (the next three chapters will discuss these three virtues).

4. *Prudence (Good Ends/Effective Means)*

As we've discussed, the *prudent* entrepreneur has the difficult job, particularly in highly competitive situations, of connecting and integrating effective means with good ends. The skills to achieve effective means include attracting customers, adjusting the product or service to meet the demands of these customers, securing resources, developing systems, building a team, and strategically adjusting to a dynamic marketplace. All of these are required for the business to first survive and eventually to thrive. Yet, to be a prudent entrepreneur also requires that we pursue through these effective means good ends for the business. The entrepreneur has to use his skills and techniques in the service not only of his own interests but also in the service of other stakeholders, of the community and of society. Skills and techniques are not merely neutral means of getting things done. Their exercise is a human act that demands a deliberate goal and measure if it is to contribute to our development as human beings.

Linking Ends and Means in a Wide Variety of Circumstances
However important the relationship between means and ends are, they do not tell us precisely what to do in particular circumstances. The ends and the means will orient the entrepreneur in a particular direction, but they do not always tell him in precise terms what he should practically do in this situation at this time. Every entrepreneur encounters obstacles along the way. Without a realistic perception of the business situation he is in, the entrepreneur will be like the captain of a war ship telling the lighthouse to get out of the way.

An entrepreneur then cannot pull out of his back pocket the list of moral principles or rules that will tell him what to do in each situation. Nor can he simply rely on a set of financial or productive techniques to plug in. There is no quick and easy formula to being a good entrepreneur. Some situations are unpredictable, such as natural disasters, events like those of 9/11, sickness, market downturns, betrayal, and so forth. All of these can have devastating effects on a business.

Because of the contingency and unpredictability of doing business, the prudent entrepreneur has to depend upon internal qualities of the soul that are acquired through experience. Some of those qualities will include:

- seeking *counsel* from others
- thinking through as much as possible future consequences (*foresight*)
- displaying a certain degree of *caution*

These qualities and others enable the entrepreneur to see the real situation as it is and not some preconceived notion of how he would like it to be. While these qualities cannot predict the unpredictable, they enable the entrepreneur to be better prepared for difficulty and to successfully navigate the challenges thrown in the path of the pursuit of his vision for the business.

Such qualities also help the entrepreneur to learn from her mistakes and deepen her understanding of ever more effective means and nobler ends. Because the development of virtue is a life-long project, it is not an act to achieve but a habit to nurture. It will entail repetition not in some mechanical fashion, but in a thoughtful patterning within one's life by which the entrepreneur's experience in his business through reflection and prayer will lead to greater growth and insight. Too often people can have the same experience over and over again, but this experience fails to deepen understanding and perfect action precisely because it is repetitive in a mechanical fashion. It is the same old same old. If experience is to be our teacher, it must have an interior reflection to it.

For example, Reell Precision Manufacturing, a small manufacturing company located in Minnesota, encountered technical problems with faster set-up times on new product runs. This particular situation with a specific technical problem turned into an opportunity for assemblers to become better skilled and for management to provide a living wage among the lowest paid in the company. A particular situation with a specific problem resulted in the development of a new way of thinking about job design on the manufacturing floor, which moved the company from, as they called it, a "Command and Control" system to a "Teach-Equip-Trust" system. The resulting savings in set-up and supervisory times and improvement in quality enabled them to think more deeply about the moral character of the wages they were providing their employees. What started as the need to deal with a technical problem (means) was transformed into an opportunity for Reell to deepen the moral ends of the enterprise.

It is this ability to see and do the good in effective ways and in a wide variety of circumstances that marks prudence. It is often the case in the process of starting and growing entrepreneurial businesses that through technical problems great moral opportunities arise. The vision of the business is often illuminated not only by sitting around and contemplating great thoughts to put on a wall, but more importantly, through struggling with the practical issues and technical problems in the business and, through this struggle, discovering how to incarnate one's principles in practice and walking the talk. The problems an entrepreneur faces are most often of a technical and instrumental nature, such as how to manage inventories, timing and staffing increases to match cash flow; how to increase quality; and how to expand market share. These technical problems can turn into opportunities for moral growth in the company, if the entrepreneur is open to them.

The TAG Story:
Financing the Start-up

The Access Group (TAG), a manufacturing engineering consulting business, grew from the basement of one of the founders into a thriving venture. The founders, Mike Brown and Charles Hagood, achieved growth through adapting to the needs of their customers and pursuing new opportunities they discovered in the market. Initially, TAG provided consulting support for businesses needing help with manufacturing process redesign and plant relocations; but over time they adapted their services to market opportunities and expanded into related businesses.

Obtaining the first client in a consulting business proved to be a significant challenge, as they had nothing tangible to show potential clients. During their initial start-up, the founders decided to save as much of their precious self-funded working capital as possible. They became classic bootstrappers. They decided to work out of Mike's basement and garage, with their PCs set up on folding tables they had purchased at Sam's Club. Charles joked that "Mike's Chihuahua became our Vice President of Security," as he announced the arrival of each UPS, mail delivery or visitor to their "corporate headquarters." Charles added, "We were broke but were having a blast. We were never worried that we'd make it. The question was when." As business grew, the partners began to get more regular paychecks; they hired more staff for the increasing workload and finally moved out of their "corporate headquarters" at Mike's home.

TAG continued to be self-capitalized as it grew, which was particularly hard for Charles, as he had a young family to provide for with most of his cash invested in TAG. They tried to learn from each success and each failure. Their most difficult decision to this point was hiring a full-time marketing professional. This was a commitment to an employee who would not directly create revenue for the company through billable hours, unlike the project managers and consultants they had previously hired. His salary would significantly increase the overhead of this small business. But it became clear to them that it was a necessary decision in order to create sustainable growth in their new business.

To this day, they have maintained a focus on keeping their overhead low as a key part of their prudent business practices. Lower overhead decreases the sales volume necessary to break even. In a start-up business, lower overhead allows a business to reach positive cash flow more quickly. In an established business, lower overhead helps the business weather the inevitable disruptions faced by all businesses.

A crucial decision for Charles and Mike was the self-funding financing of their company. Charles explains their rationale for building their company:

We self-funded. We decided early on we weren't going to take on a lot of debt. Mike and I were both somewhat conservative, he a lot more so than me, but we were both somewhat fiscally conservative and we both decided that we didn't want to go into a lot of debt. We decided that we were going to self-fund as we went. We were in our second year of business before we secured a line of credit, but we really didn't tap into it until we had been in business about two-and-a-half years. . . . We were able to self-fund through savings, and selling projects. We put all the money that we did have into the marketing and our people, so we didn't put a lot of money into other things like offices.

While self-funding may not be appropriate in all situations for entrepreneurs, it provided TAG with a good deal of flexibility to act with a greater degree of freedom to become the kind of company they wanted to be. It is important to be clear that the founders of TAG followed a path of bootstrapping not just to be efficient but also to ensure that they could reach the ends they had established for their employees and customers.

From its beginning, Charles and Mike wanted a company that reflected the moral and spiritual principles of their faith. Neither of them had any desire to proselytize others, but they were aware of the pressures of expediency—to cut corners, to get business at any cost—pressures that could intensify with outside owners. They saw self-funding as a *means* of financing, which created five conditions to build the kind of company they wanted: (1) It reduced the pressures of unrealistic financial performance by outside investors; (2) it enabled them to weather unpredictable market downturns; (3) it allowed them to more freely tithe to the community; (4) it promoted frugality; and (5) it caused them to think more clearly about the kind of company they wanted. Let's examine in more detail each of these conditions.

1. Reduce Pressure to Maximize

To Charles and Mike, one of the main advantages of self-funding and being a private firm is that they "only have themselves to please" in terms of the financial performance of their firm. They committed to each other that they would not sacrifice their principles for profits. What this has meant to them concretely was that they could act for the long-term. Charles explains that "while relocating a client company is very profitable for TAG, it may not be the best decision for the client. There have been instances when we have completed a feasibility study and concluded that a company was better suited not to relocate and rather should change some of their operations to make them more efficient." While TAG still has financial pressures, their self-funding reduces the degree of pressure for larger margins in the short-term.

The kinds of returns that venture capitalists and angel investors are looking for create pressure to grow, in fact, to grow aggressively in a shorter period of time. Equity investors seek a fairly quick return on their investments, usually about three to seven years, which are usually realized only through the sale of the business. Outside equity investment can create what we call *entrepreneurs on steroids*. It can foster an environment of the frenzied pursuit of growth for growth's sake where raising financing and meeting financial expectations become the sole means and ends of the venture.

2. Weather Downturns

There are not only the financial pressures of outside equity and debt holders, but also the unpredictable swings of the economy. By reducing the need for outside debt financing, such as bank loans, long-term leases and trade credit, entrepreneurs can reduce additional financial pressures. Charles explains that after the attacks of 9/11, TAG, like many other businesses, "went through a really bad time for a couple of years. Fortunately, we didn't have a lot of debt. We were very conservative financially, so we were able to survive when a lot of the companies that we worked with or had competed against didn't survive. We hunkered down."

As a business grows, debt financing is easier to secure. But in the frenzy of growth, the entrepreneur can take on a level of debt that cannot be sustained during the inevitable slowdowns that all businesses face. Many of the post-9/11 small-business failures were the result of funding their growth through high levels of debt financing. When the economy stalled after 9/11, debt-laden small businesses could not meet their financial obligations. On the other hand, the more prudent small-business owners, such as TAG, who had taken on little or no debt and had built up significant cash reserves, were able to weather the economic shock that followed the attack.

3. Give Freely

An important part of the mission and the culture of TAG is to not only make the lives of the partners better through the success of the business, but also the lives of their employees and people in their community. Their self-funding strategy gives them the freedom to support church-sponsored mission trips, which are a regular occurrence for TAG employees and their families. TAG pays for the expenses related to these mission projects for all employees, and in some cases their family members. TAG employees and family members have participated in three to four mission trips a year, including locations in Asia, Africa and the Appalachian region of the United States.

Charles and Mike committed from the very beginning of TAG to contribute approximately 8 percent to 10 percent of net income to charity and faith-based causes. However, even during years when the business had losses, they still gave significant gifts to charity. Both Mike and Charles view charitable giving as "bills to be paid" rather than a residual part of their profitability. In addition to mission projects, other donations go to local churches, sponsoring children who cannot afford to join youth sports programs, a scholarship fund to support working adults pursuing college degrees, the local YMCA, and other community organizations.

4. Promote Frugality

From their beginnings in Mike's basement, Mike and Charles have consciously avoided anything they considered to be extravagant spending. They have never lost their bootstrapping ways. Even as TAG became more successful, they chose to operate out of a moderately priced office space and to keep travel costs down by flying the discount airline Southwest and staying in hotels such as a Hampton Inn for Charles and Microtel for the more conservative Mike. They believe this approach to management benefits them as shareholders, their clients by keeping costs down, and their employees and the community by freeing up more resources to support charitable giving.

5. Develop a Unique Culture

Mike and Charles had an opportunity to sell TAG a few years ago, but they decided that the timing was not right. Currently, Charles isn't considering selling TAG for two reasons: First, he does not think that TAG would be as successful in the near term without their culture and without the relationships that he and Mike have with their clients. He admits that a new owner could probably make the business more profitable, but it "might not be the same business." For Charles and Mike, TAG's profitability is only part of its success. The kind of work community they develop is their principal understanding of success. Second, any sale would likely require Charles to stay on, and he is adamant that he would never want to work for anyone as only an employee.

To be prudent in a business is to aim at good ends and employ effective and sustainable means for achieving such ends. Mike and Charles have seen self-funding as one of those means to achieve the kind of company they wanted to build. While they have taken risks with their profitability, these were the prudently evaluated risks of the seasoned entrepreneur who is always trying to find new and more effective solutions to old problems. The proof that such prudence can work is that, while they took risks, their spiritual and moral orientation has served thus far not as a constraint on their profitability but as the basis of their success.

What is critical for the entrepreneur is that he is cultivated in a moral vision that prevents a crass utilitarianism while providing opportunities for humanizing the organization in new and as yet un-thought-of ways. Prudence, as a virtue, is impossible without technical and financial competency as well as a vision for a community of work where the purpose of the company promotes the dignity of each of its stakeholders and the common good of all involved. Such a purpose creates a *moral seedbed* within which dealing with practical and technical problems can turn into opportunities for expressing in deeper and clearer ways that the business is a community of work where people can develop as fully as possible.

While prudence is a key virtue during the start-up and early development of a company's culture, as we saw in the story of TAG, it also should be an integral part of how a business manages its growth. Here is a summary of some additional prudent practices.

- *Manage as if "cash is king"*: Having cash reserves allows businesses to make it through the initial economic paralysis of a major event. Thirty days' cash reserves (enough cash to cover essential and fixed expenses) would be a minimum recommendation. Even 90 days of reserve would not be too much to have at this period of time.

- *Manage overhead carefully.* Overhead pushes the break-even point of any business higher. If sales suddenly drop off for an extended period of time, a lower break-even point that results from lower overhead expenses can soften the impact of any economic shock. It takes less recovered sales to get back to break-even.

- *Avoid fixed, long-term commitments.* Any major shock on a market may require new business tactics, strategies or even models going forward. One reason the American auto industry reacted so poorly to the oil shock in the

1970s was that they had built their businesses on the assumption of a very static business model. It literally took them years to undo this model and adjust to the new reality they faced. They had to be able to react much more quickly to changing customer preferences and operate in a market with many new competitors where there had been only three.

- *Build in flexibility.* Understand that you may need to quickly undo some decisions. Make this as easy as possible to accomplish. For example, shorter term leases offer more flexibility than longer term leases if space needs suddenly change. Leasing equipment as needed is more flexible than purchasing equipment. Outsourcing certain functions to outside companies is relatively easy to undo if conditions change. However, if the business hires staff to perform that same work internally and the culture is one that tries to avoid laying off employees, the entrepreneur may feel locked in to keeping those staff longer than the business can support.

- *Watch and manage inventories carefully.* Certainly you don't want to choke your business growth, but don't go overboard with purchases either. Purchasing raw materials or other inventory using volume discounts may not be wise. Be as "just in time" with your inventory as possible.

The prudent entrepreneur understands that all businesses will eventually face financially challenging times, whether from the loss of a major customer, the aftermath of a major weather event, or a terrorist attack. The entrepreneur does not know what the exact nature of this challenge will be or when it will happen, but she knows that something, someday, will impact her business in a way that could bring the business to the brink of failure. Her prudent acts now, to manage her cash flow carefully, to not take out too much of her profits as distributions or dividends, to maintain her bootstrapping ways even as her business grows, will offer her the best chance that her business can make it back from that brink and survive whatever comes her way.

Conclusion: A Deeper Purpose

There is the often-told story of a medieval traveler who came across three men constructing a building. The traveler asked the first man what he was doing, and the man replied, "I'm building a wall." He posed the same question to the second builder who sighed with exhaustion and said, "I'm putting food on the table and a roof over my family's head." The traveler asked the question of the third builder, who responded, "I'm building a cathedral for the praise and glory of God."

What we have been attempting to make clear in this chapter is that a wise entrepreneur puts together, synthesizes and integrates worthy ends and effective means in the right circumstances. For many entrepreneurs, there will be little argument that we should have the most effective means available. Where arguments might occur is what makes up a "good end." In our relativistic society that wants to reduce this to one's personal and emotional preferences, the entrepreneur cannot be so glib and simplistic. The entrepreneur, if his enterprise is to have any substance and attraction for others, has to tap into a deeper end and purpose that connects people. Like the third builder, the prudent entrepreneur has to make clear to himself and to others that the end of his work has a moral and spiritual character. He will also have to prove to his stakeholders that he can effectively achieve these noble ends. Prudence enables him to know how to build *and why he is building.*

As we move to the next three virtues of justice, courage and temperance, we will not be leaving prudence behind. These three virtues form our desires and will direct us to the good. So we always want to keep in mind that whenever we speak about one virtue, we are always assuming that the other virtues are present. Prudence, then, is only prudence when it is connected to the moral virtues, especially the virtue of justice, which we will discuss in the next chapter. The moral virtues of justice, courage and temperance are all preconditions of the intellectual virtue of prudence. These moral virtues, as Aristotle put it, "help us aim at the right mark." What prudence does is help us find the right means to achieve the right mark.

As we will see in the next chapter, an entrepreneur who desires goals of justice for his employees, for example, through fair wages and a participatory workplace, needs the "perfected ability" to make right decisions that can sustain such goals within the context of a productive organization. Prudence informs the other moral virtues with its intrinsic characteristic of the ability to perceive and perform the good that is possible (and not possible) in each particular situation. Good intentions are necessary but insufficient.

Notes

1. Quoted from Antoine de Salins, "Does Finance Have a Soul?" http://www.stthomas.edu/cathstudies/cst/conferences/antwerp/papers.html (accessed February 2008).
2. Thomas L. Schaffer and Robert E. Rodes, "A Christian Theology for Roman Catholic Law Schools," *University of Dayton Law Review,* 14 (1988): 5-18.

4

Justice: Creating Right Relationships

Free enterprise cannot be justified as being good for business.
It can only be justified as being good for society.

PETER DRUCKER

In the company I co-founded, my partners and I were very deliberate in our discussions about the various stakeholders of our business—particularly our employees.[1] At that time the health-care industry was undergoing dramatic change. Managed care was just beginning to spread across the country. For-profit, publicly owned hospital corporations were being formed to take advantage of the growth and changes in the industry. Early on, these corporations began to get a bad reputation, particularly in how they treated their employees.

While being a for-profit company, we wanted to approach the opportunities we saw in the market in a way that did not compromise our shared values. One practice that had become common in health care was to engage in frequent temporary lay offs of employees when demand for services went down. We intended to build a culture that was in part based on a commitment to our employees.

We talked at length about the heavy burden of obligation to the employees who believed in our company enough to trust us with their labor and with their careers to help us build our business. We all agreed that our commitment to our employees was for the long-term, and we agreed to a policy of no layoffs due to short-term fluctuations in demand for our services. We would always try to pay our employees at competitive levels, which was often a strain for a new and growing company like ours. These commitments often meant that the three founders of the business would have to go without pay for periods of time during our early growth.

We also recognized that whatever success we had would be a result of our employees' efforts. We committed various programs that would allow the leaders in our company to have a share of the equity of our business. We also implemented various profit sharing and incentive programs to share the success we hoped to have in our business. One of my partners would often remind us that we should view our employees and their families as an extension of our families.

This relationship with employees characterizes the essence of the virtue of justice. Yet I was reluctant to use the word "justice." Such a word made me feel uneasy. When I heard people talking about justice, I heard *external legal constraint on the economic interests of entrepreneurs, most often imposed by the government.* I saw the term "justice" as a bully club by which entrepreneurs were made out to be the source of society's problems rather than a solution.

This understanding of justice became crystallized for me while at church one Sunday, when we received the so-called "justice sermon" from our pastor during a Labor Day weekend. It happened during a time when our health-care business was suffering from significant growing pains. Like many fast-growing businesses, we were suffering a significant cash flow crisis. We were desperately trying to keep up with our payroll, which had resulted in none of the partners getting any pay for several months. That Sunday morning, I heard about the evils of profit, the greed of businesspeople and the need for the government to constrain their unjust behavior and look out for workers.

Although there are injustices in the business world, he never mentioned the possibility that business owners could actually be virtuous in how they act. Instead, my pastor condemned business leaders as immoral and assumed that the state and all its laws were the only possible source of justice. Adding insult to injury, as I was walking out of the church, the pastor put his hand on my shoulder and said, "Jeff, I want to speak to you sometime about our new capital campaign and whether I can count on you for a commitment." Not only did I feel like I was being bludgeoned during his homily in church, but now he wanted "his share" of my "evil gains."

This story and others like it generate an understandable reservation among entrepreneurs about thinking of themselves as agents of justice in their businesses. The unfortunate outcome is that, more often than not, entrepreneurs give up on explicitly thinking about their work in terms of justice, which, ironically, strengthens the external constraints on business. If business owners fail to act as agents of justice, it most often defaults to government agencies to act. Such deferment has, in part, resulted in an average cost of regulatory compliance for small businesses in the United States of $7,647 per employee, according to a recent report from the Office of Advocacy of the U.S. Small Business Administration.

Because of the preponderance of externally imposed constraints, the entrepreneur does not develop a language or a culture of justice within his venture that can help him personalize his responsibility to share his success with the stakeholders who helped him create that success. Rather than seeing their allocation of resources as an opportunity for virtue, for creating right relationships, entrepreneurs will often see the distribution of wages, profits, prices, and so forth, as only mechanical decisions determined by some combination of regulations, market forces and economic power. Often, they see no relationship between their decisions and, indeed, their growth in virtue on the one hand and fostering a more just distribution of resources on the other.

The twenty-first century was ushered in by a renewed entrepreneurial economic engine through which we have the opportunity to rewrite the old rules and create a new order. One area that needs serious rethinking and reordering is how the entrepreneur understands justice. In this chapter, we will rediscover an understanding of justice that is consistent with a faith perspective that is more communitarian and less individualistic—where it is more about the nature and the kind of relationships that entrepreneurs have with employees, partners, investors, customers, suppliers and the larger community, and less about the protection of the entrepreneur's private property and hard-earned profits. We will focus on the meaning of justice within the Christian tradition and examine one company's struggle to establish right relationships from its founding through its compensation system. As we hope to show, justice is not some imposed restraint on the company but a natural reality that needs to be named for what it is—a search for right relationships that creates a community of work.

A Primer on Entrepreneurial Justice

Crucial for the entrepreneur is to have a notion of justice that speaks to her experience as an entrepreneur who is in the process of developing—of one who can become good in the work that she does. When we look at a Christian view of justice, we find an understanding that ennobles the entrepreneur's moral and spiritual calling, precisely because it calls forth the possibility of fostering stronger bonds of communion. Two characteristics of justice will help us begin to see the importance of justice for the entrepreneur. The first has to do with the very meaning of justice as "right relationships" and the second concerns the "distributive function" of justice.

Right Relationships

The first characteristic of justice is its ability to create right relationships. Too often, however, when we think of the word "right," we think of rights, and in particular, my *private* right to do whatever I want with my body or my property or my company. Yet, we become right and just as people not by our shouts for freedom or claims for autonomy, but when we are freely in right relation with others. This flows out of our social nature as people. We can have all the rights possible and still be wrong if our relationships with others are not fostering real bonds of community.

It should be remembered that Moses' greatest challenge was not in leading the Israelites out of Egypt, but in trying to get them to live together in a way that would foster right relationships. The exodus out of Egypt was not simply a *freedom from* slavery, which of course was very important, but a *freedom to live in community* bonded by God's covenant. In many respects the liberation was the easy part; what was most difficult was the community part. God was able to get them to leave Egypt; He just couldn't get them to live together as a faithful people in a flourishing community.

The Jewish and Christian vision of justice is not only a liberation to autonomy and independence, but rather at its heart this freedom is a liberation to community and interdependence that sets the conditions for people to become who they were created to be. We are created to be free and we are created to be responsible; thus, *we are most free when we are most responsible*. This has a strange ring to modern ears; but when we are responsible, we have the *ability to respond* to what God has created us to be, which gives us the freedom to be in right relationships with others and with God. The Old Testament refers to responsibilities that arise out specific relationships within the community: employer and employee, ruler and people, husband and wife, parent and child, and so forth. Justice, then, is an internal capacity of the person to be connected with, and give freely to, others.

The entrepreneur can sometimes fail to see this meaning of justice as right relationships because he often associates freedom with autonomy. He will use these words to tell you the reason he will start a company: "I want to be my own boss," "I want to work for myself," "I don't want anyone telling me what to do," and so forth. As important as autonomy is, the crucial issue in the Christian tradition is what kind of community you are developing, not simply how much autonomy you have. You can have all the freedom and autonomy possible and still be a lonely failure. *Free* enterprise brings with it implicit responsibilities to all who support your entrepreneurial pursuits, and it is the fulfillment of these responsibilities that provides the freedom to be the kind of enterprise that fosters a community of work. As Andrew Carnegie once said, "No man can become rich without himself enriching others."

This internal quality of justice is crucial to understand since we often think of justice as an external constraint rather than as an internal liberation of our self-interests so as to freely connect with others. Justice is an internal quality of the soul, in which the entrepreneur moves out to others—employees, customers, investors—and creates communities where people have an opportunity to flourish. In the Christian tradition, justice is considered first among the moral virtues precisely because it is others-related, not simply on an occasional basis, but as a habit of mind and heart. This inclination to give to others leads to the moral growth of both the individual and the community as a whole. We cannot be in right relationship with our employees (and workers cannot be in right relationships with their employers) unless, in the words of Thomas Aquinas, our souls are so "entirely possessed by justice" that we have the *constant* will to give others their due. This is no doubt a tall order for the entrepreneur, but without justice, his vocation is on a sandy foundation.

Institutionalized Distribution

The second characteristic of justice has to do with its *institutional distributive function*. While justice is a good habit of an individual, justice is also ordering the institutional life of its members in such a way that conditions are created for each person to flourish. Crucial to these institutional arrangements is how entrepreneurial firms distribute what they create. Entrepreneurial firms are the central institution for creating wealth in this country, but what is not always discussed is that they are the central institution for distributing wealth as well. Entrepreneurs and their firms distribute the following:

- goods and services
- jobs
- wages
- capital/dividends
- philanthropy
- taxes

Just how well entrepreneurs distribute these outcomes turns on whether they are distributors of justice or not, on whether they have sought to institutionalize in the organizational culture the virtue of justice through fair prices, well-designed jobs, just wages, capital distribution, charitable giving, and so forth.

This distributive theme is strongly articulated in the Scriptures. Christian entrepreneurs cannot escape the sense that their role as distributors of justice is an important part of living a life of faith in business; it is so important that the Old Testament (see the prophets Jeremiah, Amos, Isaiah) and the

New Testament alike (see in particular Matthew 25:31ff and Luke 12:16-21; 16:1-13,19-31) warn that our salvation may be at risk if we fail to distribute justly the resources within our sphere of influence. But unlike the prophetic homily in the story at the beginning of this chapter, entrepreneurs not only are the problem to a just distribution, but they are also an integral and essential part of the solution.

Within the Christian tradition, entrepreneurs are called to be "distributors of justice," not merely "maximizers of wealth." It is business more than government and private foundations that creates and distributes wealth. But if entrepreneurs neglect their call to be distributors of justice, they will be under the same judgment meted out to the rich man who failed to see Lazarus in his midst. It is crucial for the entrepreneur to understand that justice means both an internal habit of character and a fundamental component of the culture of the firm.

At this point, you may be thinking that this is simply too much to ask of entrepreneurs who enter the competitive and increasingly complex world of business. It is hard enough to raise capital, satisfy customers and make a profit; but to heap upon the entrepreneur a moral debt to be in right relationships may seem too much to ask. But it is precisely because business is so competitive and complex that justice is so crucial. Without this fundamental solidarity of right relationships with other people within an organization, the likelihood that entrepreneurs and their employees will shrivel into small-minded maximizers of wealth is ever greater. This is why the entrepreneur needs to pray on a constant basis the following prayer:

So guide us in the work we do
that we may do it not for the self alone,
but for the common good.[2]

It is this sincere commitment that helps an entrepreneur develop the habit of connectivity with others, to see that his work as an entrepreneur is critically important to the common good.

With these two characteristics of justice in mind—right relationships and distribution—we need to explore what justice looks like in entrepreneurial firms. The challenge for us is to see how justice operates within a business venture. As we will see, this is more ordinary than one might think.

The Reell Story: Creating Right Relationships

More often than not, as we saw in the opening story about Jeff's business, the word "justice" is not one that comes to mind for an entrepreneur starting a new business. But if we understand justice as creating and establishing right relationships, we begin to see that this is precisely what many entrepreneurs intend to do—and many do so because of unjust situations they were exposed to early in their careers as employees.

Many entrepreneurs start their companies because they feel constricted in a corporate setting. They feel constrained and limited by its culture. What is often lacking for the aspiring entrepreneur working in a corporate setting is right relationships with other employees, with customers, with suppliers, and even with family members. And so they leave to start their own business, which they hope can have the culture they envision.

When Dale Merrick, Bob Wahlstedt and Lee Johnson started Reell Precision Manufacturing (RPM), all three were engineers who came from 3M in St. Paul, Minnesota. While they had great respect for 3M as a company, their individual situations in the company made it difficult for them to feel that this was the place for them.

For Bob Wahlstedt, successful executives at 3M too often paid the price of family estrangement for career advancement. He could see that the more one progressed up the proverbial company ladder of success, the more one had to sacrifice other relationships, including family and friends. Bob's notion of success did not include a discontented spouse and troubled children. Bob was particularly close to his own father and he was hoping for and expecting the same kind of good relationship with his future children. The longer he was at 3M, the more he became uneasy about where he was heading. In a rather gradual and at times imperceptible fashion, the culture of the company was affecting and changing him, and the changes were not what Bob wanted. Bob thought he could have it all—career opportunities, strong family bonds, good relationships with his employees, and so on. But it was becoming clear that a gap existed between thought and reality.

These three men left 3M because of relationships, not because they wanted to make more money. Actually, the concern about money was motivating them to stay at 3M, not leave it, since their salaries were generous and there were no guarantees that their new business would ever provide them with comparable incomes, or for that matter, would even succeed.

What these three men really wanted were relationships that nurtured their souls at work, that created community and that made the world a better place. So when they started their company, they listed four complementary aims for their new company:

- to earn a living
- to grow personally and professionally
- to be able to put family first
- to integrate faith and work

The founders of Reell also asked themselves a very important justice question: "Can we deny our employees what we value so much for ourselves?" If the three of them desired security, strong relationships with family, and integration of their faith and work, wouldn't other employees want the same? The founders of Reell began to create conditions within their new business venture that fostered right relationships with those in the company. It was their intent that this would serve as the basis for the personal and professional growth of their employees. By designing better jobs through training and skill development, promoting a culture of participation and ownership, committing themselves to livable wages, having a "last alternative" layoff policy, developing family-friendly policies, and being dedicated to high-quality products and customer service, the leadership at Reell created the conditions for a community of work to take place.

While these activities do not guarantee right relationships in themselves, they do create the conditions in an organization for all employees to see a common life together, a life of interdependence. And while never perfect and always in need of revision, the founders of Reell believed that the fruit of a work community is manifested in an extremely low turnover rate among employees, a high number of applicants for each job opening despite a tight labor market, a spirit of sacrifice when economic hard times occur, and the best quality product in their industry.

Here we come to one of the profound insights of justice and one of the more overlooked natural laws of morality. An African proverb begins to get at this natural law: *A person becomes a person through other persons.* No person, whether entrepreneur, doctor, pastor or carpenter, can develop as a person if she is only concerned with her own interests. Her growth as a person is dependent upon the growth of her relationships with others. If the founders of Reell had denied their employees *what they valued so much for themselves,* the founders would have denied for themselves the very deepest values they prized. If their work did not create the conditions for others to develop, they would have paradoxically stunted their own personal development.

Just Wages

Our focus in this section provides an example of how entrepreneurs can begin to build a culture of right relationships through compensation. Our intent is not to say that this is the only means of building right relationships in an entrepreneurial venture, or even the most important means to this end. Rather, we are trying to offer a specific, concrete example. Reell Precision Manufacturing's policy on just wages illustrates the richness and depth that can be achieved through such a program. We will explore some other practices at the end of this section.

One of the most effective statements on the meaning of a just wage comes from a Protestant clergyman in the early nineteenth century by the name of Charles C. Colton. He wrote:

> *Our incomes are like our shoes;*
> *if too small, they gall and pinch us;*
> *but if too large they cause us to stumble and trip.*

Colton's statement reveals a very simple truth. Wages, like most things in life, can be either excessive or defective. Just because market forces can determine a wage rate, such forces do not give the wage any magical status as to its moral worth. There are countless examples of excess of executive salaries and the "stumbling and tripping" that result. There are even more examples of workers trying to get by on sub-living wages, especially among those who are unskilled and uneducated, and the galling and pinching that results in their lives.

In 1996, Reell had to face the pinching of wages within their company. In an employee survey, the leadership of Reell had to come to grips with a very strong message from those assemblers on the manufacturing line: "We love working at Reell, except for the pay." What they didn't like about the pay was the amount. At $7 an hour, it was not enough to make a decent living. But Reell competes in an industry where $7 is the going rate for assemblers. To pay them anything more would create a competitive disadvantage for the company. But because of their commitment to establishing right relationships, the leadership had to embrace the problem, which can be summed up in the following manner:

- *Market Wage:* The actual market wage for assemblers in the company was $7 an hour ($14,000/year).

- *Living Wage*: In 1996, their estimate of a living wage in St. Paul, Minnesota, was $11 an hour ($22,000/year).

- *Gap*: How could they make up the $4 an hour discrepancy between a living wage and a market wage?

The founders and management of Reell desired to pay their employees not only their market worth, but also the worth of who they were as people (persons made in the image of God who deserve to meet at least a minimum of their needs). However, they were all too aware that their customers would only pay a market price for their products. If Reell paid $11 an hour to its employees while competitors paid $7, their cost disadvantage would almost assure that they would lose many, if not all, of their customers. Realizing that the *ought* of a living wage always implies the *can* of a sustainable wage, the company had to seriously rethink how it was doing business and find a creative means to implement this aspect of building their just culture.

This rethinking was premised on three principles that should guide the distribution of resources: need, contribution and order. For Reell's founders and management to be in right relationship with their employees, these principles would need to be robust enough to both create a community of work *and* be fiscally responsible. The principles can be summarized in the following way:

- *The Principle of Need and a Living Wage:* A wage that fails to meet the needs of an employee (in particular, an adult employed full-time) is a wage that will struggle to carry the weight of a real relationship. In order for this relationship to flourish, an employer must recognize that employees "surrender" their time and energy and so cannot use it for another purpose. A living wage, then, is *the minimum amount due to every independent wage earner by the mere fact that he or she is a human being with a life to maintain and a personality to develop.*

- *The Principle of Contribution and an Equitable Wage:* While the principle of need is *necessary* for determining a just wage, it is *insufficient* by itself, since it only accounts for the consumptive needs of employees and does not factor in their productive contributions to the enterprise. Because of effort and sacrifice as well as skill, education, experience, scarcity of talent and decision-making ability, some employees contribute more to the organization than others, and are due more pay. An equitable wage, then, *is the contribution of an employee's productivity and effort within the context of the existing amount of profits and resources of the organization.*

- *The Principle of Economic Order and a Sustainable Wage:* Pay is not only income for the worker; it is also a cost to the employer, which has a significant impact on the

economic order of the organization. Without the foresight of how a living and equitable wage will affect the
economic order of an organization, a just wage becomes a high-sounding moralism that is impractical.
A sustainable wage, then, *is the organization's ability to
pay wages that are sustainable for the economic health of the
organization as a whole.*

These principles enabled Reell to embrace at least three bottom lines to a just wage. First, Reell's management resisted the
common practice of passively delegating their responsibilities
simply to the mechanical force of labor markets. They saw
themselves as moral agents, as distributors of justice in the market place and in their community. Nor were they simply working toward a target wage because they thought it would attract
and retain employees who would make the company more money.
While paying better wages enhanced morale at Reell, since employees witnessed a commitment by management to establishing right relationships, management's inclination was to
continue to focus on their concern for their employees' needs.

Second, what enabled Reell to pay a living wage was a whole
new way of doing work at the company. Reell redesigned their
assembly line from a Command-Direct-Control style management (CDC), where management and engineers made all the
decisions concerning the conception of the assembly area, to a
Teach-Equip-Trust (TET) style of management in which employees were taught inspection procedures, equipped with quality
instruments and trusted to do things right on their own assembly line. Employees decreased set-up times for new products,

reduced the need for quality inspection, increased overall quality and required less supervision. By reducing these costs, the company not only was able to set pay rates at a level closer to a living wage, but they also created a richer work experience by making employees accountable for developing their knowledge and skills. They found that this did just as much, if not more, for right relationships than increasing hourly pay.

Third, Reell's management realized that every action has a reaction and that raising wage levels without changing the work process would have serious consequences on their cost structure. To simply pour surplus profits into wages without any consideration of how to strengthen the performance of the company undermines the company's ability to pay living wages. Rather, Reell was able to shift much of the cost of inspection and supervision from overhead expenses into part of the direct cost of their hourly workers.

What became clear for Reell's management was that low wages were merely a symptom of a much larger problem of how the company worked. When work is designed to use $7 of talent, it is difficult to pay people anything more than that amount. Prudence dictated that the living, or target, wage could not come automatically. The reason the company called it a target wage was that it was something to be worked toward. When an employee is hired with no experience and no skills, the company pays the worker the market rate ($7 per hour or whatever it is at the time), but then makes a commitment to move that employee to the target or living wage ($11 per hour) through training and skill development. So as employees learn the skills and gain experience, which Reell provides, their pay goes up accordingly. Both sides have the responsibility to create justice in the working relationship.

There is more to be said about how Reell's mission guided its decision-making on wages, but it is important to be clear where the company's responsibilities lie in light of the Christian social tradition. This tradition does not hold Reell (or any firm) responsible to pay employees in excess of a sustainable wage (a wage consistent with the sound financial management of the firm), even if that wage falls below a living wage. To do so would unjustly place Reell—and all the firm's employees—at risk of economic failure. In a market economy, no firm can be obligated to pay without regard to labor costs' effect on its competitive position, since that would amount to an imprudent choice leading to economic failure for the business. To "impose" justice in this manner is doomed to long-term failure. Nevertheless, the founders and management of Reell do have a moral obligation to create right relationships with employees to work *toward* a living wage. This is why Reell can pay less than a living wage so long as it is working toward correcting the situation through some set of means such as training and skill development.

It is also important to point out the responsibilities of employees here as well. Employees are not merely recipients of justice, but they are also an integral part of the process of creating right relationships in how they choose to pursue their work. Employees have to develop their knowledge and skills not only to increase their pay, but also to improve the competitiveness and performance of Reell. If they don't continuously learn and develop in their work, they fail to give their due to the company. When Reell implemented the target wage, they had to fire

117

some employees because they either would not or could not fulfill the training in statistics and quality. Such firings were just, since the employees were failing to uphold their part of what constituted "right relationships." All work, including the work of employees, is an ongoing continuation of God's creation. They, like entrepreneurs, are responsible for good work and need to be held accountable.

Other Just Practices

As we noted at the beginning of the last section, this example of a just-wage policy is an illustration of only one possible practice of justice with one specific stakeholder. We developed this example in greater detail because we wanted the reader to see the nuances of what a wage policy would look like informed by the virtue of justice. There are other practices that can help entrepreneurs reach the goal of a just culture.

1. Participation in Equity

Acting justly compels business owners to acknowledge that profits and the increase in value of their businesses are not their doing alone. Employees at all levels, and particularly those with decision-making authority, all contribute to the success of a business. Therefore, all who contribute to success should benefit in some way with the rewards that come from financial success. Inviting employees to share in the equity of an enterprise is tricky business. We cannot go into all the complications and their pros and cons here. We can, however, note some of the ways that entrepreneurs have practically tried to operationalize equity sharing.

Phantom Stock (sometimes called Mirror Stock) and Stock Appreciation Rights (SARs) are two tools now available to entrepreneurs. Phantom Stock is a formal promise to pay a bonus at a specified period of time to employees as if they owned a certain amount of stock based on the increase in value of the company using a predetermined method of valuation. For example, let's assume that Sally had 1,000 "shares" of Phantom Stock that was valued at $10,000 when she was entered into the Phantom Stock program where she worked. Under the plan at her company, there was a valuation of the business each year, which was used to calculate the Phantom Stock bonuses. If the value of the company increased by 10 percent in the first year, she would get a bonus check for $1,000 based on the number of Phantom Stock "shares" that she owned. SARs work in a similar way, except that after a vesting period the employee bonuses can be exercised at any time by the employer rather than at fixed times like the Phantom Stock plan. These plans go further than simple profit-sharing incentives (which are a valuable tool that many companies now use) since they not only recognize short-term profits but also long-term gains in valuation that establish a means to share in the creation of wealth.

Another way to share the equity is through Employee Stock Ownership Plans (ESOPs). In the U.S., approximately 11,000 companies now have these plans, covering more than 8 million employees. As a financing device, an ESOP turns labor workers into capital workers, which in turn links the structures of ownership with social equity. ESOPs can also foster among employees a greater connection with their company that can increase personal initiative leading toward greater productivity and efficiency, and less waste. CEO of Springfield Remanufacturing Company (SRC), Jack Stack, brings this point out in favor of his company's ESOP. In his view, employee owners tend to reorient themselves to the whole question of what it means to benefit from the company. They think of "sacrificing instant gratification" for long-term stability and longevity. Stack explains that if "you have equity and understand it, you know why it's important to build for the future. You can make long-term decisions. You will pay attention to the day-to-day details, but you're doing it for the right reason: because it's the best way to achieve *lasting* success."

2. Employee Emergency Assistance Funds

Some forms of distributing justice can involve more than just the entrepreneur. Employee emergency assistance funds allow co-workers to contribute money or days off (i.e., sick days, leave days, vacation time) to a pool that can be used by employees who face an emergency. Often, employers contribute a match to this pool or may commit to replenishing it if the funds run low due to unusually high levels of need. These pools can be administered by a committee of employees who evaluate requests from co-workers to determine if the situation merits assistance.

The Lee Company provides residential and commercial heating and cooling, plumbing and electrical services. They employ hundreds of workers in mostly blue-collar positions. Bill Lee, the company president and third-generation owner of this family business, wanted to be able to offer more to his employees. They have a broad pay scale ranging from those who start at an entry level with no skills all the way up to engineers and

other professionals. Especially for lesser-skilled younger workers, a financial crisis can be devastating. Lee explains that "if
they have a health insurance claim that's not covered or they
have an unexpected death and they have funeral expenses, it is
a real crisis for them. So we felt that we could set something up
that would keep our folks from being financially devastated,
and also let the employees be involved in helping one another.
Employees put the money into our Lee Employee Assistance
Fund for their co-workers. It is not just the company doing
something for them, but it is the workers doing something for
one another." An emergency assistance fund helped the Lee
Company to not only distribute justice in the company at a
practical level, but it also helped to create a culture with a
strong sense of justice in how employees treat each other.

3. Equal Benefit Plans for All Employees

A common practice in many businesses is to have stratified benefit plans, based on employee classification. Benefits may be
structured differently for hourly versus salaried employees, ex-
empt versus nonexempt, executive level versus all other employees below the executive level, and so forth. The Lee Company has
chosen to give all employees the same benefits package no matter what level in the corporate hierarchy their position falls
and no matter what form of classification a specific job carries.
In doing so, the Lee Company employs another practice that
helps them create a just culture. Bill Lee explains:

> In our company, we have had a long-standing tradition
> of not having a different set of benefits for our field

employees than we do for our office employees. A lot of companies do have dual benefits; office workers get this, field workers get that. And there are certainly things inherent in their jobs that are different for field and office workers. But one of the things that we have tried to do is keep the barriers broken down so that people feel like the $9-an-hour, low-skilled entry level worker is just as valuable to this company as the CFO. The entry-level employee's benefit package is the same as the CFO's. He is treated as fairly and justly as anyone else in the company.

While justice does not always mean giving everyone the same thing, giving all their workers the same benefits package has provided the Lee Company a strong sense of social equity within the company, contributing to its sense of community.

4. Just Firings

Because of shifting markets, cultural fit, performance concerns and the like, there are times within an organization when employees need to be dismissed. At times, not to fire people is more unjust than firing them. Tomasso Corporation, a privately owned company in Quebec, specializing in the production of frozen dinners, utilizes a practice that fosters right relationships between managers and those who are dismissed. Managers who lay off or fire an employee must meet with that employee at least two times within a year after the dismissal. The reasons for this practice are multiple, but principally, management needs to follow up on a difficult and painful decision to be sure the employee is all right and to see if he needs further help. Another important reason for the practice is to give the manager and employee the opportunity to reconcile differences, which is necessary to foster right relationships even with those who no longer work with the company. The effects of unreconciled relationships can be like a wound that never heals and is vulnerable to infection.

A Final Caution: The Ditches of Injustice

As we have pointed out throughout this book, the virtue tradition tells us that we are prone in our actions to either excess or defect, two ditches that we call vices. In terms of *excess*, one of the dangers of incorporating justice as it relates to wages and benefits is that sometimes justice can be distorted into entitlement. It is not born out of any sense of justice as right relationship but as an excessive attempt to take care of one's own needs to the detriment of the financial health of the venture. This excess can be found in employees wanting greater pay without the hard work of enhancing company performance. The entitlement mentality has been something that Reell has had to manage.

In terms of *defect*, the entrepreneur is often "allergic" to the word "justice." He places his faith not in the relationships of those he works with but in markets that will somehow reveal that all will be well. As one person we know put it, "If I believed in God as strongly as certain people do in the 'free market,' I would be a mystic." In a similar way, there are others who place their faith in the government to make things right. But whether it is the market or the government, both of these positions distort the capacity of the entrepreneur to act justly. We call this the vice of omission, since it neglects the entrepreneur's unique capacity to create right relationships in the distribution of the resources of the enterprise. This distribution is not a mechanical decision or a legal obligation, but rather a responsibility to become a distributor of justice.

Notes

1. This example is told from Jeff's experience.
2. The prayer for Labor Day from *The Episcopal Book of Common Prayer.* http://www.sacred-texts.com/chr/bcp.txt (accessed February 2008).

5

Courage: Taking Risks to Achieve Good Ends

God, grant me
the serenity to accept those things I cannot change
the courage to change the things I can and
the wisdom to know the difference.

<small>REINHOLD NIEBUHR, "THE SERENITY PRAYER,"
AKA AN ENTREPRENEUR'S PRAYER</small>

Of all the virtues covered in this book, courage is most commonly associated with the entrepreneur. It is the courage to take the plunge and launch a new business venture, to endure great pressures, to attack complex problems, to overcome significant obstacles and rest only when sleeping.

This quality of taking risks and enduring the difficulties of such risks—what we might call the entrepreneurial impulse—is crucial to the dynamism of our economic system. Without it, our economy would stagnate and decline. Yet, while there is often a tremendous excitement when starting a business, particularly when it meets with initial success, difficulties are inevitable, and this adversity can be wearing. Technical problems don't always find simple, inexpensive solutions. Working capital can suddenly dry up. Customer needs can rapidly change. Key people will quit. Misfortune and adversity can crush the spirit of the most energetic and creative entrepreneur.

When entrepreneurs are in the muck of building a business, getting their product off the ground, attracting customers and building up cash flow, these are times of real temptation to simply give up on the initial vision and go back to the safety of a 9 to 5 job.

These emotional ups and downs are common to most entrepreneurs; but to understand what is actually happening in these experiences, we need to be mindful of two necessary characteristics that define courage. First, as we've already mentioned, courage is the habit of taking risks and enduring hardships. The second characteristic, which often gets overlooked in the popular press, is the *ability to direct risk-taking and endurance to good ends*. It is the goodness of the end that determines when to stick at something, how much to sacrifice, and when, ultimately, to give up.

Entrepreneurs go into business for a variety of reasons. Financial rewards are certainly among them, but it is rarely the only reason, and often not even the primary reason. Many entrepreneurs have within them a desire to do something great, as we have seen in many of the stories in this book. They want to contribute to society; they want to see their product and service make the world a better place. Yet, when the real world of running the business begins to reveal itself, entrepreneurs can easily retreat from this moral vision. Feeling overwhelmed by adversity, the entrepreneur is tempted to restrict his concerns to survival issues and retreat from the difficulties of a grander vision for the enterprise. While entrepreneurs will often describe these feelings as being overwhelmed, they rarely describe them as temptations of retreat, fear or vulnerability; consequently, they rarely describe these times of difficulty as opportunities to respond courageously.

However, when the *virtue* of courage enters his or her understanding of specific circumstances, the entrepreneur is better able to resist the temptation of restricting the enterprise to only an economic outcome and see more clearly that at its core the enterprise is a moral and spiritual reality. What is helpful in all this is when people can name these fears, doubts and temptations, and see how the virtue of courage can be a response to such difficulties.

How Courage Gets Side-Tracked

Entrepreneurs tend to fall into these temptations in one of two ways. The first temptation has to do with a focus on *having*, whereupon they give up on a larger moral vision that was with them when they first committed to starting their venture. When this happens, entrepreneurs settle upon defining courage only in terms of economic success. Courage becomes a habit prized for its attainment of external or instrumental goods rather than building a culture where employees grow, customers' needs are met, communities develop, and the common good is fostered. With a focus on *having*, courage becomes silent on the means the entrepreneur uses to strive toward the vision, and success is narrowed to include only the attainment of external ends, such as wealth, power, honor or fame.

The second temptation has to do with a focus on *doing*, where the end of courage is primarily described in terms of the achievement of overcoming major obstacles and enduring pain and difficulty. What is interesting when one listens to certain entrepreneurs is how they talk to each other of their "doings." The focus sometimes is less on what was accomplished and more on the effort and pain that led to the accomplishment. In growth seminars for entrepreneurs led by Jeff, it was common for the participants to share their stories of Herculean efforts—the 90-hour work week for more than a year, the sleepless nights, the family sacrifices and break-ups, deterioration of health, and so forth. For many it almost seemed to be their badge of honor.

The problem with these two temptations is that the *end* of entrepreneurship is reduced wholly to a financial order or toward a show of Herculean entrepreneurial effort—what might be termed "work for work's sake." Creating wealth and human endurance are necessary components of a good entrepreneur, but they are not rich enough categories to describe the good in the entrepreneur. Within this view of entrepreneurship, other ends, such as sharing the wealth, creating products and services that serve the common good, developing the moral character of the entrepreneur, building a strong culture that creates a community of work or finding spiritual meaning in one's work, are ignored.

This deficiency of ends within entrepreneurship begs for an engagement with a rich moral tradition that allows one to persist willingly in the face of fear and pain for the sake of *good ends*. Because courage is directed to a good end, it will always be dependent upon other virtues, especially the virtues of prudence and justice discussed in chapters 3 and 4. These virtues help the entrepreneur discern his own achievements and goals in light of an end that enlarges and expands his notion of the good the more it is sought. Courage, then, is perfected by its connection to the other virtues.

In this chapter, we will examine how the internal quality of courage helps the entrepreneur overcome these temptations of *having* and *doing*. We believe that courage is of particular importance for the entrepreneur, because it directly engages an entrepreneur's self-understanding as a risk taker. To start and sustain a business often involves major obstacles that threaten the economic survival of the business. When taking such risks, one encounters the possibility to either turn risk-taking into the virtue of courage or into a vice of recklessness or cowardliness.

A Primer on Courage and Risk-Taking

To understand courage for the entrepreneur in the Christian and Western tradition, we need to be clear on its relationship to *risk, fears* and *the good*, otherwise we fall into the temptations described previously.

"Courage" is the word used to confront the universal human experience of feeling vulnerable in front of an unknown future. Without this feeling of vulnerability, courage would not be necessary. To be vulnerable is to be at risk, and to be at risk is to open oneself to harm or loss, as well as to development or gain. To make this point, Josef Pieper explained that an angel cannot be brave, since it cannot be vulnerable. This insight is an important foil to the commonly heard statement that *good ethics is good business,* which is often translated as *doing good will lead to greater profits.* This so-called truism in business circles rings somewhat hollow in the face of courage. It is hollow because courage is removed before the business even starts. If doing good always leads to profitability, then there is no risk for the entrepreneur, since there is nothing possible to be lost through moral behavior. While doing good often leads to increased profits, there are times when it does not. Thomas More (1478-1535), the great saint and statesman from England, became the second most powerful person in his country because of his virtue. He also got his head chopped off because of it.

Besides being empirically unverifiable, such a cause-and-effect statement that good ethics lead to more profits tempts us to be like the gods, to have certainty over a future that is beyond our control. Our quest for certainty, for a risk-free future, is an understandable impulse, but one that is ultimately misguided, because people and the world are contingent realities. While science and technology have helped us see a bit further into the future, the complexities of how people interact with their environment create so many variables, so many possible scenarios, that our formulas for prediction will always come up short.

Business, and especially entrepreneurship, is an adventure, which means the future is unknown and in doubt. We can certainly manage risk, and we can reduce our risk, but we cannot eliminate risk. We are not angels, fortunetellers or gods. We are human beings, and part of our predicament is that the future remains partially hidden from us. Risk means that the future is unknown, and we can never be sure that our moral, or for that matter immoral, behavior will guarantee fortune.

This risk, this vulnerability, this daring of the future is what an entrepreneur has to face. The question is, How do we face this future? In our vulnerability of the future, we are tempted, usually through fear, to avoid situations and opportunities that we know we ought to approach. Fear inclines us to forfeit some greater good, such as a vibrant community of work, in order to hold on to a lesser good, such as greater profits. Profit is obviously good, but the entrepreneur too often pulls the trigger of layoffs, downsizings and other cost-cutting measures before their time. His fear of loss can distort his reasoning abilities, damaging another good, such as employee morale. If he were more mindful of the emotional influence of fear, he would realize the importance of courage in confronting his fear.

Courage, however, is not the same as having no fear. Fearlessness, which is often seen as a quality of courage, is actually the result of a misapprehension of reality. Some people are unaware of legitimate fears because they lack knowledge of the situation or are simply foolhardy. They are blind to the potential dangers at hand. There are others who fear nothing because they love nothing. The person who does not fear death is often the person who has lost the will to live. It is often from this deficiency of love or from a dull mind that fearlessness results in reckless action.

Fear is an emotional response to a particular situation and, like other emotional responses, it is an expression of our desire for things. Our emotions suffer a certain excess or defect, because emotions by themselves have no internal compass that regulates and disciplines them toward a good life. Through excess, we take too many risks, fight battles that do not need to be fought, and end up damaging others and ourselves unnecessarily. Through defect, we accommodate ourselves too easily to difficulties, shrug off persistent evils and fail to take up the opportunities for good while building a profitable business.

This understanding of fear helps us understand two kinds of entrepreneurial risk. The first is the one that is most often thought of in association with entrepreneurial endeavors. It is the *risk of failure*, or what is sometimes called "sinking the boat." This is the risk that can come from excess and fearlessness. Luke Wooten, founder of Station West Studio, explains that while people have "to take a risk, it's got to be a calculated risk. It would be very unwise to go out and say, 'I'm going to go out and build a big recording facility because that's what I want to do,' when you've never engineered a session." Many entrepreneurs have sunk their companies because of an emotional recklessness—following a dream that had little grounding in reality.

The other type of risk in entrepreneurship arises from the *risk of defect*. This risk is associated with what economists call opportunity costs or "missing the boat" risk. It is failing to act on what is really a sound opportunity. Charles Hagood, cofounder of The Access Group, explains that "we weren't as aggressive in the very early days as we probably could have been. I think we didn't realize all we had to offer. I think we lost a lot of opportunities in the very early days, not recognizing what was there."

"Missing the boat" does not refer only to the risk of missed business opportunities; it also refers to missed moral opportunities to build good companies. Thomas Aquinas called this

132

moral missing-the-boat risk "meanness." He described mean-ness not so much in terms of doing wicked things, but in terms of *doing small things when one should be doing great things*. Aquinas defined evil and sin as the absence of good. Sin chips away at the fullness of the good that business can do and leaves us with a bland and uninspiring vision of maximizing profits.

Dee Hock, former chief of the Visa bank card operation, de-scribes this problem in a similar way. "It's not that people value money more but that they value everything else so much less—not that they are more greedy, but that they have no other val-ues to keep greed in check."[1] God has called us to do great things in this world, and we too often settle for the conven-tional standards of success. Yes, profits are a good and neces-sary thing, but they are not good enough. We suffer too often from a failure of nerve to offer the world a robust notion of the good that business does. Instead, often out of fear, we settle for a conventional and thin notion of the good that has no capac-ity to inspire greatness, nor resources to overcome our fears.

Too often we risk ourselves for small things that are too limited, such as money, fame, power and status. They are lim-ited because they fail to develop and engage the fullness of the human person. This is why a person needs other virtues, such as prudence and justice, because there is a difference between a proper willingness to endure pain and overcome fear and a proper recognition of what is genuinely good. While enduring pain is one quality of a person of courage, if it is done for the wrong reason, the habit becomes a vice because of the end cho-sen. To be courageous is to place oneself at risk for the good of others. This is why the Herculean efforts of entrepreneurs do not necessarily qualify as courage; they seem to suggest that the entrepreneur's effort—and nothing else—is the sole criterion of a courageous act.

In light of this understanding of risk, fear and the good, the courageous person is someone who may feel fear because of the unknown, but whose convictions toward the good keep his fear from overwhelming his judgment in action. Courage, then, is the habit that helps us respond in a way that directs us to see the whole.

In the next section, we introduce Jim Stefansic, an entrepreneur who, in starting a venture, is currently wrestling with the typical issues of courage. The obstacles he is facing are not being overcome simply by a set of skills or formulas but by his internal qualities of virtue, along with a community of people who can help his enterprise stay the course toward building a faithful enterprise.

Opportunities for Courage

A new business goes through four basic phases: pre-launch, start-up, growth and transition to new ownership. This journey, as we have pointed out, is complicated by the challenges of when to start the business, how to raise capital, manage cash flow, develop operating systems to handle growing demand, address morale problems due to the stress of changes in the business, maintain a culture that reflects the entrepreneur's values, and deal with interpersonal relationships, including partners and family tensions. In this section, we will discuss the first two issues of our list, *taking the plunge by leaving one's job* and *raising capital*, and examine the importance of risk-taking and courage.

Before co-founding Pathfinder Therapeutics, Dr. Jim Stefansic had been a successful researcher at Vanderbilt University. He was part of a research team developing a new application of image-guided surgery for patients with liver cancer. In standard liver surgeries, a large incision is made through the chest and abdomen to expose the surface of the liver. Either a wedge or entire segment of the liver is removed to clear the organ of its tumors. Open liver surgery has an average five-year survival rate of 35 percent to 40 percent when tumors are confined to the liver. As more and more of the liver is removed, however, five-year survival rates drop significantly due to loss in liver function. The image-guided surgery, which his team was working on, would provide more precision in removing all of the tumor and cancerous cells while leaving as much of the healthy liver tissue intact.

While pursuing an MBA at Belmont University, Jim was presented with an opportunity. Angel investors were willing to provide the seed funding needed to take this technology out of the lab and make it commercially viable. In addition to having market potential, this technology offered the possibility of saving many lives, as it could significantly increase the number of patients for whom surgery would be an option and increase the survival rates by decreasing the amount of the liver that would have to be removed during surgery. It could allow for many more patients to become candidates for surgery to remove tumors and thus have the potential to beat their cancers. This move presented Jim with a series of choices.

The first choice for Jim was whether or not to make the jump into the new business. To make the business work would require Jim to leave his faculty position and take the personal risks associated with launching a high-risk business. While Vanderbilt was a prestigious place to work and do research, there was something about the academy's theoretical and research character that did not fit Jim. He wanted to build something, not just research it. No doubt the security of an academic position and a constant paycheck had great appeal, but Jim was itching for something more from his work. This something more would entail an economic risk, but Jim was also mindful that there was an emotional risk of staying at Vanderbilt and regretting not starting Pathfinder. In other words, he was aware of the missing-the-boat risk.

Another dimension of Jim's first step out of academia and into the intensity of starting a business was his wife, Candy. The new venture was not only his decision; it was not only his risk. His first and most important partner in this decision was his wife. At the time of the decision, Jim and Candy did not have children, and Candy was working. Financially, the decision for Jim to leave Vanderbilt was hedged by her work. Candy was not only supportive of Jim's decision but also encouraged him to make the move. She knew that Jim would not be satisfied as a researcher. She also saw the importance of the technology he was developing to improve patients' lives.

For many entrepreneurs, launching a business is the single most courageous act. It requires the courage to act on the dream. Courage requires risking the pursuit of the upside returns, the wealth and the entrepreneurial experience in the face of possible bankruptcy that can include a loss of wealth, personal assets and even one's reputation. This is the step that many potential entrepreneurs fail to take due to fear of what failure may bring, as well as fear of the potential cost that success may require of them.

Even those who do start a business may carry this fear with them as they begin their businesses. Starting a business often requires quitting a good-paying job and using one's home as collateral for business loans. It also requires a commitment to long, hard hours of work and irregular paychecks. On the surface, Jim's situation may not seem as dramatically courageous as that taken by some entrepreneurs. But he did quit a good-paying job, and he is now working much longer hours with unpredictable pay. He is now doing things for which he has had no training or preparation, moving from a research project that is life-saving into an operating business venture. This is courage.

Another important choice for Jim was the decision of investors in the company. As he moved forward in starting Pathfinder Therapeutics, a major focus of his time was spent finding other venture capitalists to further fund the business. It is important to point out here that Jim's risk was in leaving the security of an academic position, not in risking his home and life savings. Many entrepreneurs find people to share the risk in starting new ventures, especially ones that entail a great deal of technology costs. To attempt to put all that risk on oneself can be more reckless than courageous.

The search for financing proved more challenging than Jim had anticipated. When he pitched the imaging product to venture capitalists, especially to the larger ones, he was struck by their lack of interest in the product. Most of them were totally focused on high returns and short time frames. What worried

Jim was not the focus on returns and time frames; he, too, was interested in making money on this project, for himself and for his investors. What worried Jim was the one-dimensional focus on financial returns. Did he really want to partner with people who had little interest in the life-saving dimension of this product? While he needed the capital, was he taking on too much *risk* with a venture capitalist who was only concerned about the numbers and who could not see the whole?

As Jim traveled the country looking for capital, however, he began to find that not all venture capitalists were the same. The longer he searched, the more he found venture capitalists who were asking questions about the technology and its contribution to the medical field. Although few in number, these venture capitalists not only had a financial logic, but also a product logic. Jim connected with them precisely because they could see the whole and not merely one part of the business. However, one of the challenges with these more holistic venture capitalists was that they tended to be smaller firms that did not have deep enough pockets to cover the full costs of his funding needs.

As we write this book, Jim is still facing risks in finding not only enough capital, but also finding the "right" capital. The decision is still up in the air and we do not know which combination will be the best one. Yet, as Jim goes through all the complexities, all the unknowns, all the changing variables, what he does have is a vision with which to face such risks. As we've already pointed out, entrepreneurs are not gods. They cannot predict the future. In their vulnerability, their principal constant is the vision they have to help them make such decisions.

An entrepreneur's business vision includes three main elements. First, the vision includes *a mission statement,* which is the definition of the product/service the business produces, the market for which it is produced and any specific and unique aspects of the business that will give it a competitive advantage (such as technology, customer orientation, and so forth). The Pathfinder Therapeutics mission statement reads as follows: *To develop innovative, image-guided surgical systems that allow physicians to perform more efficient, accurate therapeutic procedures and improve patient outcomes.*

Second, the vision goes beyond the more objective description in the mission statement to include the *core values and principles* that will guide the business. The founders of Pathfinder Therapeutics used their statement of creed to communicate their core values:

We will operate with honor;
we will operate with intelligence;
we will operate with compassion;
we hope to operate with wisdom.

It is through the moral framework that the entrepreneur begins to address the deeper dimension of why he or she is in business. More specifically, this vision shapes the opportunities pursued, the people chosen as business partners, the people hired, the decisions regarding products and markets, whether to grow and how fast to grow, the corporate culture, and the entrepreneur's engagement with the community as a leader and/or citizen.

Finally, the vision incorporates the entrepreneur's *aspirations of hoped-for outcomes*. An entrepreneur's definition of success can go well beyond profit maximization to include a whole range of other factors, including employment in the community, the ability to create balance with family, the ability to bring a needed service or product to the market, or creating a certain work environment for employees that is not available in other businesses.

In Jim's case, it is his vision that will help him decide which venture capitalists will invest in Pathfinder. This is not a formula that guarantees a right decision. It is wrought with vulnerability and danger and possibilities of excess and defect. Jim needs a great deal of courage informed by prudence and justice to choose the right investors. His vision serves as headlights on a dark road, giving him enough visibility to drive, but not enough to know what's beyond the bend.

Conclusion: The Nobility of the Mundane

By now you might be thinking, *Okay, I can see that Jim Stefansic is acting with courage, but he is dealing with a life-saving product; most entrepreneurs are not producing life-saving products.*

It's possible to over-romanticize courage and fail to recognize the nobility of the mundane. Bob Wahlstedt, the entrepreneur in chapter 4, told us that he wished he could have built something that saved lives, such as a cardio pacemaker, instead of the clutches for copiers and hinges for laptop computers that he does build. Yet the common good entails so much more than just life-saving medical devices. The infrastructure necessary for a functioning society that allows people to develop will entail a multitude of products and services, including hinges and clutches, bolts, tables, chairs, steel, toilets, plastic, roads, as well as pacemakers, imaging medical devices, social services, computers, and so forth. In other words, we cannot be overly romantic about how we define the good that business does. It takes a lot of products and services to make a good society run, and in the creation of these various products, people are also being formed.

This is similar to the mother and father who underestimate the importance of their parenting to the common good. The mother and father who endure the daily routine of bringing up their children to be good practice courage just as much as the missionary who endures the hardship of poverty in the developing world. In a similar way, entrepreneurs who make hinges or plastic molds or nuts and bolts in a way that fosters quality products and helps employees grow practice courage through their endurance to resist such market pressures that foster cheap products, instrumentalize employees and ignore communities. In the daily grind of dealing with unexpected problems, trivial issues and monotonous practices, the entrepreneur will be tempted to give up the vision. It is precisely at these moments that courage is needed to continue the vision that is founded in prudence and justice.

These temptations are not unique to entrepreneurs. They are common to anyone who attempts to build relationships in marriage and family, the classroom, the church, and so forth. What is helpful is when people can name these fears, these doubts, and see how courage is critical at the various stages.

By viewing a business over its life cycle, we can begin to understand the distinct issues, challenges and decisions that arise at each stage, especially those involved in starting a venture. To strive to be a good entrepreneur, one must understand that these challenges call for more than just technical solutions. They also draw from the moral qualities of the entrepreneur. But the entrepreneur cannot build a good business alone. He must also build a community of people who can help the enterprise stay the course toward good ends as the business evolves.

Note

1. Dee Hick, quoted in John Kavanaugh, *Christ in a Consumer Society, Still* (Maryknoll, NY: Orbis Books, 2000), p. 11; see also http://www.maryknollmall.org/chapters/1-57075-666-X.pdf.

6

Temperance: When Is Enough, Enough?

~~~~~~

First the man takes a drink, then the drink takes a drink,
then the drink takes the man.
JAPANESE PROVERB

Watch out for the dangers of an excessive activity, whatever . . . the job
that you hold, because many jobs often lead to the "hardening of the
heart," as well as "suffering of the spirit, loss of intelligence."
ST. BERNARD'S ADVICE TO POPES IN THE TWELFTH CENTURY

Of the four virtues, temperance would seem to be the most out of place for the entrepreneur. Whereas temperance is viewed as a virtue of moderation and balance, the successful entrepreneur is excessive, driven, passionate, single-minded. In many ways, temperance seems more like a vice than a virtue for the entrepreneur.

For example, a gifted computer specialist named Peter came to Jeff for assistance in getting his cash flow and financing under control. He had identified a market niche for a computer application in the engineering field that he had been developing with his previous employer. The employer was not interested in the idea, so the entrepreneur gained permission to take the idea and start his own company to develop and market the product.

Peter methodically refined the concept and made the software application operational and ready for market. He reported that he was on the verge of breaking into the market but was "dealing with some financial difficulties." If he could raise a little more money he would be able to make the business sustainable. When asked how bad his financial condition was, he matter-of-factly stated that he had funded his start-up primarily through his life savings (i.e., cashed his retirement accounts) and a second mortgage on his home. He had gotten "a little behind" on his loan repayment and lost his house. In frustration, his wife took their children and left him. And, oh yes, he was about to have his car repossessed, which is where he had been living since he lost his house. "But," Peter said, "I only needed to raise another $50,000, and then I could deliver my product to several customers." He eventually did raise the funds and did become financially successful.

This story is not an uncommon one for entrepreneurs. Their work brings out a certain flow, a rhythm, a sense of being connected and alive, that other activities don't seem to give. Work brings to them a great deal of pleasure, satisfaction and self-esteem. Yet, like all desires, when does an entrepreneur's desire to make his enterprise successful cross the line from being a healthy passion to an addiction that disorders other important aspects of his life? One of the more difficult moments for an entrepreneur is to recognize when enough is enough.

This failure to recognize when enough is enough stems in part from the real pleasure of moving an idea into reality. Most of our pleasures tend to be more consumptive in nature: food, drink, sex, wealth. But there is also a wonderful pleasure in creating an enterprise from scratch based on an idea. It is precisely the pleasure of the work that leads entrepreneurs into the temptation to disorder all other good, such as marriage, family, health, friendships and religion, in the achievement of their businesses.

In light of this description so far, some may think of "temperance" as another word for "balance." But we have to be careful to not equate the two, although they are related. At its best, balance helps us make time for our family. Bill Lee, president and CEO of the Lee Company, gives a good example of this balance: "I create boundaries for myself and work. If I had traveled and was gone for a night or two, I would stay home in the morning until my kids were gone. I'd spend time with the kids and then with my wife, and then go to work late." If one does not make time for family and other leisurely activities, temperance will not be achievable. As the book of Genesis tells us, we are not only made to work, but to rest as well (see Gen. 2:2).

The deeper question of temperance informed by the Christian message, however, is not only "a break from work" but also how we rest and what we rest in. Balance does not answer these questions. Neither does a sequential response help. Some entrepreneurs fall into the trap that rest will come once they are successful. "I'll rest and even be a philanthropist once I make my millions." "I'll rest when I'm 40, or 60" or whatever age somewhere in the future. Temperance challenges the entrepreneur that such sequencing of life, and even balance, is not enough. We need a deeper *integration* between our work and rest, which the virtue of temperance fosters.

A Primer on Temperance

To understand the importance of temperance for the entrepreneur, we need to take seriously a couple of points on how we view our desires, passions and feelings in terms of the moral life:

- Our desires move us to act. This is the way we are hardwired.

- We have varying intensities of desires depending on our physiological makeup and the way that we were brought up.

- We feel our desires before we are able to think about whether they lead to good or bad situations.

- If we simply act on a desire without a reasoned idea of a good end, we suppress other desires and become enslaved to the particular desire.

- Our desires will lead us to a good life depending on how they are ordered.

- Our future desires are partly formed by how we order and respond to our desires today.

In light of these points, we can come to a working definition of temperance: Temperance is a habit of self-restraint in our desires for certain goods *so as* to order our lives to a more comprehensive and much larger set of desires that will lead to a good life. Chocolate fudge caramel cheesecake is a good, but if I don't restrain myself from the second and third pieces on a habitual basis, I begin to sacrifice my health through clogged arteries and obesity. Alcohol is a good, but if I don't restrain myself from additional drinks, I begin to act stupid and sacrifice good friendships, and my own health. Work is a good, but if I don't restrain it, I begin to neglect relationships with my family, friends and God.

Temperance helps us see the importance of saying no. Our nos clarify the yeses of our commitments. This is one of the reasons why the Ten Commandments have negative prohibitions, not because God wants to keep us from having fun, but because clarity on our nos helps us see the limits of the goods of the earth. Temperance is not simply a puritanical repression of the good things of this world, but a habit that orders our passions to a good life. Temperance is not a suppression of our natural inclinations or desires, but a habit that provides us the capacity to follow all of our desires in a more holistic fashion. It does not silence our desires; it channels them into our deeper moral and spiritual desires to serve the common good and God.

For example, our no to pornography says yes to fidelity. The Internet, for example, has shown us how powerful sexual desires are, and how tragically that good can be distorted through pornography. Pornography disorders the good of sexual pleasure by preventing it from developing the higher good and pleasure of lifelong relationship by reducing the sexual good to only a physical sensation. In actuality, pornography represses the sexual good from its inherent relationality in the moral and spiritual realms and creates unhealthy and ultimately unpleasurable sexual relationships. Sexual desires have the capacity to contribute to intimate and profound relationship, but only when those desires are ordered toward a lifelong commitment founded in marriage. Outside of this context, it tends to be driven by selfish gratification that distorts relationship.

In a similar way, our desire to work, to make something, has the capacity to contribute to a real community of work where a group of people overcome their inborn egocentricity and make something that contributes to a better world. Outside of this end, work becomes either mere drudgery or an exercise of egoism.

Without temperance—the ordering of our desires toward the good—our passions begin to dictate behaviors that actually make us slaves. While the alcoholic is free to drink, we know that once he takes the first drink, the drink has now taken him, and he is no longer free, but addicted. Rather than having our passions control us, as Peter did, illustrated at the opening of this chapter, we control our passions by being able to order them to the good. This temperance is a sign of a free person.

Temperance is a form of self-control of our appetites, which are prone to excess as well as defect. But the reason why temperance is so important here is that the restraint leads to a proper ordering of our desires that enables us to lead a good life. The restraint we need to curb eating and drinking is not done because these desires are bad, but so that we can order such desires to a fuller life and enjoy the goods as they should be enjoyed.

We all know that food, drink, wealth and sex become less enjoyable the more addicted we become to them. Our excesses of these goods eventually provide us less pleasure, but ironically, our craving for them becomes fiercer and fiercer. While the first scratch of an itch provides great relief, each subsequent scratch becomes less and less pleasurable, but we still scratch. We know that joy will not come through these limited, but real, goods, but we too often keep them at the price of our own misery.

Here we come to a deeper reality of our faith, which temperance helps us understand. Jesus tells us in the Gospels over and over again that we cannot find ourselves unless we deny ourselves (see Mark 8:34). We need to have a certain element of sacrifice, of giving over ourselves, if we are to find a deeper desire, a deeper joy to life. In the Christian tradition, a genuine and authentic sacrifice reflects a self-gift that involves a certain loss but will nonetheless fulfill rather than repress the person who makes the sacrifice. Italian religious activist Chiara Lubich, the founder of the Focolare Movement, explains this point in a very simple experience: "[When] I have a flower and I give it away, certainly I deprive myself of it, and in depriving myself I am losing something of myself (this is non-being); in reality, because I give that flower, love grows in me (this is being)."[1]

We cannot stress enough the importance that *desire is not the problem*. Rather, the problem arises from how we order our desires. In one of Thomas Aquinas's prayers, he prays, "Grant, oh merciful God, that I may *ardently desire* . . ." It is a prayer that we may desire rightly, because our desires are such an important part of our moral and spiritual life. Too often we pray to repress certain desires, but we should pray for the desire to do the right thing. This is why a virtuous action, in order for it to be virtuous, must include not only doing the right thing but also desiring the right thing. While doing the right thing when one does not desire to do it is a noble action, it does not reach the perfection of virtue. To act only *from* passion will disorder the good; but to act *with* passion will bring out the fullness of the good.

Here we come to the heart of temperance. Temperance directs the "inner order" of the human person by overcoming our disordered desires through a comprehensive set of desires and passions ordered to the common good and God. While our desires for food, drink, work, wealth, fame and sex are powerful desires, they are not the only desires within us. We desire lifelong relationships, authentic communities, and the opportunity to contribute to the common good, to name a few. Our most intense and profound desire is friendship with God. All of these desires can get repressed by our immediate desire for physical pleasure and personal comfort, as well as from a culture of consumerism and careerism. Temperance helps us order our various desires toward a more comprehensive set of goods that create a good person, a good entrepreneur, a faithful company. Internally, temperance begins to provide us a deep sense of an integral human life—of integrity.

Workaholic Entrepreneur

For an entrepreneur, one form of intemperance is expressed through workaholism, the inability to see that work is a part of a whole life, and not the whole of life. Workaholism is the disordered habit of finding comfort in work to the neglect of other important activities and responsibilities. For the entrepreneur, workaholism has become part of the social mythology of the entrepreneur as hero. With his focus on achievement, work becomes a form of addiction that disables the entrepreneur from seeing that there are times when the business needs to be tempered, if not at times even sacrificed to the cause of family or health or other larger goods.

Author Rabbi Jeffrey Salkin points out that work is the only socially acceptable addiction in our culture. While most people are loath to admit their addictions to alcohol and drugs, the addiction to work is often worn as a badge of honor. The danger for the entrepreneur, precisely because the vocation is so important, is that an addiction to work will exhaust his identity through his work. The entrepreneur is never just an entrepreneur; he is also a parent, spouse, citizen, church member and, most profoundly, a child of God. In terms of wealth, the apostle Paul wrote that money is not the root of evil, but the *desire* for money is, and in particular, the *disordered* desire of money and wealth (see 1 Tim. 6:10). While there is nothing wrong with the desire for wealth for the sake of living well, all of us face the temptation, especially in our consumerist society, to exchange a rational pursuit of wealth with an anxious desire for wealth.

This disorder often happens in gradual ways for entrepreneurs. One entrepreneur we know, who founded an environmental consulting business, caught the wave in the early 1990s of increasing environmental regulation. As his business grew to 500 employees, he began to gradually lavish himself and the company with bigger offices, more expensive furniture, finer dining and higher salaries. Each step up in expenses became the baseline of expectation for him and the company. But as the competition heated up—and this is an inevitable reality that every entrepreneur should prepare for—the market began to shrink and his expenses outgrew his revenue, causing the company to downsize and lay off, which caused him and his company significant pain. He learned the hard way that frugality and simplicity are important virtues allied to temperance, virtues that would have enabled him to live within his means and prepared him for a shrinking market.

While an excessive desire for wealth can corrupt the entrepreneur, what is even more dangerous for the entrepreneur is the addiction to the work itself, as indicated in our opening example. Entrepreneurs, when they achieve a good deal of success, are quite susceptible to the vices against temperance. Success breeds pleasures, and such pleasures tend to be sought with greater and greater intensity, which results in an addiction to work. Some studies have indicated that work addiction may even have bodily addicting chemicals such as adrenaline, non-adrenaline and endorphins, resulting not only in great highs at work, but also withdrawals during leisure, such as headaches, depression and other side effects.

One of Freud's disciples, the Hungarian psychologist Sándor Ferenczi, called this the "Sunday neurosis."[2] He found that the Sunday neurotic (or for the Jewish patient, the Saturday neurotic) would develop a headache or a stomachache or an attack of depression often on Sunday afternoons. Some have argued that these symptoms may be a result of dread of going back to work. But Ferenczi concluded that his patients were suffering from the Sabbath, that their rest was resulting in boredom, emptiness, disease, precisely because their rest lacked any spiritual enrichment connected to contemplation and community.

This inability to rest may be one of the most significant spiritual dangers for the entrepreneur. While one of our principal questions throughout this book for the entrepreneur is "What am I working for?" the entrepreneur also needs to ask, "What am I resting in?" If she fails to ask that second question and provide an answer that connects to who she is created to be, the entrepreneur becomes rest*less*.

Josef Pieper called this restlessness by its Latin name, *acedia*. He defined it as an inner restlessness, a roaming unrest of the spirit that creates a rootlessness to one's life.[3] For the entrepreneur, this restlessness is often channeled in going to the next opportunity, always thinking the next win will provide fulfillment, always hoping the next enterprise will satisfy the restless heart, but always finding restlessness returning, often with greater intensity.

Acedia haunts entrepreneurs in powerful but often unconscious ways. While their enterprising spirit may have the look of being purposeful, optimistic and in control, the work of entrepreneurs infected by this vice may be merely a distraction from their loss of meaning, from the void of their interior life that leads them toward seeking satisfaction through work. This *acedia* is often camouflaged by other virtues such as diligence, industriousness and creativity, which hide a symptom of a deeper problem of rootlessness. While diligence and industriousness are important virtues for any kind of work, they become vices when these habits serve as a means to escape oneself through excessive work that crowds out all other dimensions of life.

What often underlies an entrepreneur's addiction to work is a deeper loss of purpose beyond work. The entrepreneur will often rally others to work harder and smarter and use the phrase "Work and don't lose hope." But hope in what? The entrepreneur will work for greater profit, larger market share, higher productivity, more fame, more achievements, but he will have lost any sense of a greater purpose. Like the person who is trying to convince others how much fun he is having, the entrepreneur realizes that inside, he feels empty of meaning.

Two characteristics of this *acedia* are boredom and anxiety. *Acedia* produces boredom not in work but in everything else but work. There is the deepest curiosity in every technical aspect of work, but a failure to wonder about himself not just as an entrepreneur but also as a human being who is part of a larger world sharing a common destiny with others.

Acedia also produces severe anxiety when the entrepreneur leaves his venture. In an insightful article in *Inc.* magazine, this anxiety is attributed to Philip, who built a successful business only to be faced with venture capital-induced unemployment. This traumatic event produced severe anxiety, but the source of the anxiety was unclear. His psychologist Ben Yalom explains that Philip "had no financial concerns; the severance package he accepted was generous, and decades of careful investing were paying off. No, it was something else: the removal of work uncovered the bare scaffolding of his life. Like many work-driven people, Philip had few other interests. How would he fill the chilling vacuum of free time?"[4]

So how do we ensure that our life has meaning both inside and outside of our work as entrepreneurs? We believe that the following practices can be helpful to overcome this *acedia* and lead not simply to a balanced life, but to one with greater integrity and unity.

Practices of Temperance

Temperance, in a paradoxical way, restrains our desires so as to protect and deepen them. For example, while physical attraction and sexual feelings will bring us together to our future spouse, these are not enough to keep us together and can often lead to self-destructed relationships if such feelings become the basis of the marriage. In a similar way, while hard work will bring initial success to our enterprise, hard work is not enough to give us lasting and meaningful success in our work. What, then, is necessary for the entrepreneur to temper the potential all-consuming desire for work?

What is needed are practices that foster temperance in our work. These practices will initially restrain our work habits of perseverance, diligence and industriousness, but in the end they will deepen the passion and purpose of our work as entrepreneurs. We would like to highlight these practices using three categories that we believe will foster habitual temperance within the entrepreneur. We call these three the habits of solitude, of celebration and of service. These habits are important because they express an awareness of a reality that is not always evident in the daily experience of an entrepreneur's work and enterprise. We often experience our best insights not when we are in the midst of the daily grind of work, but often when we are detached from our work, not consciously thinking about the task at hand. Work, by itself, does not have the resources within itself to give the entrepreneur the meaning necessary to understand its goodness and vocation.

Solitude

The *habit of solitude* and daily silence is advocated by nearly every major religion. As the Scriptures tell us: "Be still and know that I am God" (Ps. 46:10, *NIV*). What will destroy the soul most assuredly is constant busyness and activity, along with a set of emotional tapes playing in our head that equate our identity with the achievements of our work. If we fail to put these tapes on pause, it will be very hard to hear the wisdom that deafens every fool. What needs to be fostered, especially for the entrepreneur, is an internal silence that has the ability to stop the emotional tapes of Herculean feats, illusions of grandeur, the unappreciated genius and self-pity. All too often the entrepreneur thinks of himself only as an entrepreneur. He has created mind-tapes of his achievement that he rehearses throughout the day.

While internal silence can take many forms, daily inner silence is a profound form of prayer that stops the tapes of achievement, control and self-esteem and moves the entrepreneur to a state of being able to receive the world rather than achieve one more set of goals and objectives. This state of receptivity, of being at rest, provides a clarity and honesty of ourselves and the world that is usually lost in the noise of the day. One method for settling the mind into silence is centering prayer. This prayer is a discipline that stops our work and our emotional tapes (our thoughts), and opens us to a deeper sense of self, one who is a receiver and not only an achiever.

Thomas Keating explains centering prayer in the following process, which should take 20 minutes:

1. Choose a sacred word as the symbol of your intention to consent to God's presence and action within.

2. Sitting comfortably and with eyes closed, settle briefly and silently introduce the sacred word as the symbol of your consent to God's presence and action within.

3. When engaged with your thoughts, return ever so gently to the sacred word.

4. At the end of the prayer period, remain in silence with eyes closed for a couple of minutes and conclude with an Our Father.[5]

Most likely, the more you resist this practice, the more you need it. If this practice feels like a waste of time—if it feels useless, boring and unfocused—such feelings are often telling you more about yourself than about the practice. It is telling you that you are restless, that you define yourself by doings rather than by being, that you cannot receive what you have not achieved. These rather negative feelings are graces that can be transformative if accepted as a self-critique rather than as an indictment on the practice.

This daily habit of solitude and silence outside of work can also impact the work of the entrepreneur by helping her incorporate silence throughout the day, which creates the conditions to overcome impulsive decision-making through greater reflection. We suggest three ways that this can happen:

1. *Silence before important decisions*: Silence slows time, restrains work and quiets both the mind and the soul. This allows us to enter important decisions with a sense of peace, calm and, hopefully, greater wisdom.

2. *Silence before meetings.* This can be done individually or collectively. Several companies that we know of, especially at executive and board meetings, will begin the meeting in silence.

3. *Silent Rooms*: At Ouimet Industries, each location has a room set aside where employees can be alone in interior silence, relaxation, reflection and, if desired, personal and silent meditation and prayer.

Celebration

The *habit of celebration* and weekly Sabbath are affirmations that this world is worth our commitment because it is good, because it is created. In reference to the Sabbath, Abraham Heschel has explained that "the goal is not to have but to be, not to own but to give, not to control but to share, not to subdue but to be in accord."[6] The celebratory dimension of the Sabbath is the time in which we *see* and *affirm* our end, which penetrates ordinary reality. What the Sabbath tells us is that one stops working not when the work is done, but when it is time to stop working. The Sabbath begins not on our time, but when the sun goes down, and this is something we have no control over. It is God's time, not ours. This lack of control can be difficult for the entrepreneur.

In a talk we gave to some Christian entrepreneurs, the topic of the Sabbath came up, and in the middle of the conversation, one of them sheepishly raised his hand and said, "I hear the importance of the Sabbath, but I see Sunday as my competitive advantage. It is the day that allows me to get ahead of my competition, because I am working and they are not." In the conversation, another entrepreneur challenged him and said, "Why don't you just try not going into work one Sunday and see what would happen?" His response was that he was afraid of what would happen on Monday. For the seven-day-a-week entrepreneur, the work is never done, so there is a tendency for him to never stop working, never cease to produce, and ultimately, never rest in anything beyond his work.

Besides the Sabbath, the good entrepreneur practices temperance by protecting the celebration of family time. We suggest two ways:

- *Dinner time is sacred time.* Cofounder of Reell, Bob Wahlstedt, told us that he would rarely miss dinner with the family. This sometimes meant that he would have to go back into work because a shipment needed to go out. What allowed Bob to make a commitment to his family was a unique leadership structure they called the triad—the three founders acting together as the decision-making body. This triad leadership structure allowed more time for their families, although it meant less income. While this triad structure is quite unique and unusual, the entrepreneur has to build a team he (or she) can trust that enables him to leave his work without being worried about it. This is easier said than done, but partnership and leadership structure create conditions that make temperance more likely to be practiced.

- *Family time is unmovable.* Luke Wooten, founder of Station West Studio, explains that there are certain non-work moments that require just as much if not more scheduling importance: "I try to schedule things, schedule family time that can't be moved. When you have a tracking session, you've got seven musicians there. That's something you can't really move because there is a lot of money being spent at that one point in time; and as far as the viability of a project, that's when it's all going down. I've got to create those types of things for my family as well. I've coached eight seasons of soccer. You schedule that time and make it something that you can't move."

These moments of celebration outside of work can also impact the kind of celebration an entrepreneur has in his enterprise. Most companies will have celebrations at work that celebrate performance: the highest salesperson, the most productive manager, and so forth. While they serve their role in terms of rewarding hard work, if they are not complemented by other celebrations, they send the message that profits are the highest value in the organization. Some companies have established celebrations that are particular to their culture. With its mission as "restoring people to health," Medtronic holds an annual Holiday Party where the company brings in patients and their physicians to tell the employees of Medtronic how its product has restored them to health. Earl Bakken, the founder of Medtronic, explains that the Holiday Party is "the most important day of the year for Medtronic. It is the day when we realize the true meaning of our work throughout the past year and the reason why we all work so hard to help the patients we serve."

At Tomasso, they give a yearly Prize from the Heart, which is awarded to an employee that everyone acknowledges as a model of generosity, helpfulness, solidarity and fraternity. To win the prize, a person also has to show exemplary job performance; but what is celebrated is the unique virtue that he or she contributes to making the company a great place to work. A committee of employees chooses the winner.

Service

The *habit of service* means going to the margins to be with those who are unproductive, who lack power but who have another sort of power over us, unlike any other that confronts who we really are. These are people who, on the surface, do not seem able to do anything for us, but who actually can do more for us than we can for them. Jean Vanier, the founder of the L'Arche Community, which incorporates the mentally handicapped into society, explains that "if we remain at the level of 'doing' something for people, we can stay behind our barriers of superiority."[7] We share most deeply with people when we are truly *with* them, and not just doing things *for* them, especially those who are most vulnerable and marginalized.

Many companies express this habit of service in the oft-quoted phrase "we need to give back to the community." At The Access Group (TAG), co-founded by Charles Hagood and Mike Brown, an important part of their mission is to not only make their lives better through the success of the business but also to make the lives of those around them better by giving back. Church-sponsored mission trips are a regular occurrence for TAG employees and their families. TAG pays for the expenses related to these church-sponsored missions projects for all employees, and in some cases, their family members. TAG employees and family members have participated in three to four mission trips a year around the world, including Asia, Africa and the Appalachian region of the U.S.

While these practices of *silence, celebration* and *service* initially restrain work, they actually help the entrepreneur see more clearly what is happening in his work and also the kind of person he is becoming in the work that he does. These habits foster temperance by restraining the impulse that fulfillment will come only from harder and more intense work.

As we said above, this restraint is not to eliminate the passion for work, but rather to nurture it so that it grows in a healthy way. Like the pruning of a tree, we at times need to cut back in order to see growth. This is no easy task for those of us brought up on a heavy dose of consumerism, athleticism and careerism. Yet these habits enable us to hear God's call, not usually through a new kind of experience, but rather through a new kind of insight into the experiences we have been having all along.

Conclusion: Work Is Third

While the work of entrepreneurs creates an array of goods and services that fuel a vibrant and dynamic economy, there has also been an underbelly of broken marriages, alienated children, severed friendships, neglected spirituality, increased ulcers and heart attacks, and destroyed character. All too often, our culture will excuse the underbelly of entrepreneurial success because of the good that is achieved through increased employment, increased tax revenue and general economic development. But to gain the whole world and lose one's soul is an unacceptable state of affairs (see Mark 8:36).

We close this chapter with a reflection from Jason Harwell, founder of Rebuilt Records, who recalls the difficulty, yet the importance, of a proper ordering of priorities that is necessary to live a life of temperance, which places work in third place:

I have to realize that I can't do Rebuilt 24 hours a day. It's just not healthy. So it has been a little bit of a challenge to carve out time that is just off-time, that is time for me to take care of my family. To me, it is the Lord first and then the next most important thing in my life is my family; so Rebuilt is a strong third, but it is third. But keeping it there is not always easy. And I can't say that I have been awesome at it. But at the same time, it really comes down to setting those priorities. Because ultimately I feel like the success of Rebuilt really comes from the success of us as individuals, as [we relate to] people in our lives. If we are walking with the Lord like

we are supposed to do, and we are taking care of our
families and the things we are supposed to do there,
then everything else is going to be good.

Notes

1. Chiara Lubich, "Toward a Theology and Philosophy of Unity," *An Introduction to the Abba School* (Hyde Park, NY: New City Press, 2002), p. 33.

2. Judith Shulevitz, "Bring Back the Sabbath," *The New York Times Magazine,* March 2, 2003, pp. 51-53.

3. Josef Pieper, *The Four Cardinal Virtues,* translated by Richard and Clara Winston, Lawrence E. Lynch and Daniel F. Coogan (Notre Dame, IN: University of Notre Dame Press, 1966), p. 200.

4. Ben Yalom, "Life in the Balance" *Inc.,* February 1, 1998. http://www.inc.com/maga zine/19980201/863.html (accessed July 2007).

5. Thomas Keating, *Open Mind, Open Heart: The Contemplative Dimension of the Gospel* (New York: Continuum, 2000), n.p.

6. Abraham Heschel, *The Sabbath* (New York: The Noonday Press, 1951), p. 3.

7. Jean Vanier, *Community and Growth* (New York: Paulist Press, 1989), p. 186.

PART THREE

The Good Company

Seeing Things Whole: Overcoming the Problem of Drift

Lord, enable me to seize good opportunities, be accurate in analysis,
correct in conclusion, candid with my investors, just with my
employees and honest with my customers. Stand beside me in my
work so that I will not, in order to gain a profit, lose my soul.

AN ENTREPRENEUR'S PRAYER,
ADAPTED FROM A PRAYER BY THOMAS MORE

Our journey through the four cardinal virtues highlights several fundamental insights about how to bring our businesses to life:

• *The virtues help us understand more deeply how we operate.*
The cardinal virtues are not a random list of characteristics of the person. As humans, we are thinking (prudent), willing (just) and passionate (courageous and temperance-based) persons whose success at work depends upon aligning our minds, wills and passions toward good ends with sound and effective means.

- *The virtues involve a unity—in order to have one virtue you have to have all of them.* The entrepreneur, for example, can't say, "I am courageous in my risk-taking, but justice does not suit me." This attitude undermines courage. The virtues blend together, like the ingredients of a finely prepared soup, in a way that they can never be pulled apart and taken one without the other.

- *The virtues enable us to see things whole.* The danger for all of us is that we see only the parts and not the whole. In pursuit of investors, profits, markets, customers and efficiencies, we can lose sight of the deeper human question of the end: "What am I working for?" The virtues build qualities within us to resist the temptation of only seeing profits or power or fame and will connect these limited goods to larger and more human ends.

- *The virtues move us to act with deeper levels of integrity.* As we mentioned in chapter 1, we tend to compartmentalize our lives into discrete units with no overarching unity. The virtues confront this division and move us to a unity and integrity of life. In Latin, "integrity" comes from *integritas,* where we get the word "integer," a whole number. Integrity is about being whole, the ability to order the parts of our life, overcome our division and become whole human beings.

The Christian tradition uses the language of virtues because they reveal to us a fundamental reality about our faith: God has created us to be a certain kind of people, but we are not there yet and the habits we choose will either move us toward this person or not. The virtues are those habits of mind, heart and action that lead us to continue to grow in the work we do.

We all know that it's easy to choose bad habits, especially at work. These habits lead to experiences of "the same old same old" and the mindset of "been there done that," "does it really matter?" "let's get on with it" and so forth. These habits of the mind stall our growth as human persons. They create in us cynical and sarcastic attitudes that foster spiritual and moral blockages that keep us from the good to be done in our organizations. These attitudes lead not to virtues, but to vices of pride, envy, greed, anger, despair, laziness, and more. In order to counter these vices, which are infectious in organizations, virtues are needed to move the entrepreneur toward becoming ever more complete. This completeness that unifies the virtues sees the whole and not merely the parts and seeks deeper levels of integrity.

Building a Good Company: The Challenges of Drift

While there are many challenges to practicing these virtues, we have found that entrepreneurs often stumble when they move from the *personal* to the *organizational*. One of the great challenges for the entrepreneur is how to create a venture in which these personal virtues of the entrepreneur are translated into organizational habits that build good and faithful companies. It is the transformation of the personal virtues of the entrepreneur into an organizational culture that assures that as a company grows, these virtues will be infused in all that takes place there. Just as the entrepreneur must institutionalize the business practices he has developed into systems that others can follow, so too must the practices of virtue be institutionalized in the shared culture of the business.

Yet the entrepreneur will often hesitate here: "Am I imposing my beliefs on others?" "Maybe faith needs to be kept private?" "Will I be perceived as proselytizing?" These are good hesitations, since the entrepreneur is increasingly becoming a public person who is leading people who are not like himself. But such hesitations taken too far can paralyze the entrepreneur so that he does not draw upon his moral and spiritual center. He is no longer creating a distinctive and unique company that invites others to draw upon their center; instead he or she is creating a company that tells all who enter to leave their moral and spiritual resources at the door. These hesitations hit the entrepreneur especially hard when he is moving from a small company to a larger sustained business, where policies tend to get created.

What we need to face is how the good entrepreneur creates a faithful company as he transforms the business from a small entrepreneurial start-up into a sustainable business. Important and difficult decisions are made in this period of the business. As a start-up begins to grow, it takes a steady hand to keep it going in the right direction. There are strong temptations to let the venture *drift* off course throughout its life cycle. We need to take time to describe these drifts so that we don't get stuck in them.

Vision Drift

Entrepreneurs may start their business with the intention of guiding it with a strong and noble vision, but they can lose their way in the midst of the day-to-day challenges of managing a growing business. They begin with a clear vision of what the business will become. But along the path of growth—with all of the challenges that growth creates—the entrepreneur and her employees can lose touch with this vision. We call this *vision drift*. Most often it is not a specific decision to change direction, but the result of inattention to the essential elements of the original vision of the company.

John Ward, in his study of family-run businesses, provides a helpful distinction between functional versus foundational principles or values that help us to understand the kind of vision an enterprise will develop. He explains that non-family (and we would also include non-entrepreneurial businesses) often base themselves on functional values such as profits, teamwork, innovation, creativity and industriousness. These values are obviously important to running a business, but they don't touch the person in any profound fashion. Nor do they provide any kind of distinctive vision to the business itself.

Family-run and entrepreneurial businesses are often founded upon a richer understanding of principles that are more *foundational* and that often connect to the deeper meaning of the person. These families and entrepreneurs connect their existence as a business to their family, which often, although certainly not always, entails a faith dimension to it. These businesses focus on virtues such as prudence, justice, courage and temperance as well as principles of human dignity, the common good and solidarity. This is often why entrepreneurial and family businesses have powerful and distinct visions; they have been drawn from deeper moral and spiritual principles in how they operate.

When entrepreneurs drift from this foundational vision, they have hauled in the anchor of the habits and attitudes necessary to be faithful to such a vision. They also begin to make small decisions that in their entirety move the business away from its original vision. This drift in the small decisions can be seen more clearly if we categorize them in three aspects of vision: stewardship, identity and mission.[1] Understanding these three areas and their relationships helps the entrepreneur to see the whole organization and the virtues necessary to build a community of work. We turn to these three areas and not only describe the nature of these drifts, but also suggest practices that seasoned entrepreneurs have used to prevent such drifts so as to be faithful to their vision.

Stewardship Drift: Growth for Growth's Sake

As we explored in chapter 3, *stewardship* focuses on how entrepreneurs secure and utilize resources (human, financial and material) to develop a stronger enterprise. The good entrepreneur sees himself as a steward, a trustee, an inheritor of wealth whose role is not only to preserve what he has been given but to increase such wealth, not simply for his own gain, but to make the company stronger for the future (see the parable of the talents, Matt. 25:14-29). Two crucial dimensions of this stewardship, although certainly not the only ones, are how profits and efficiencies are managed. Does the organization have adequate profit margins? Does it carefully monitor its resources with a commitment to its sustained viability, such as current cash and investment balances, cash flow from future operations, additional borrowing and fund-raising? Is it efficient in its use of resources? Does it continually seek to improve the quality of its service? Is it creative in doing more with less? Does it drive out waste? Without adequate profit margins and effective processes, organizations fail to get stronger and eventually lose hope to build for the future.

While there are many reasons for a company to drift away from its stewardship responsibilities, we have found that the temptation of "bigger is better" tends to trip up the entrepreneur. One of the first challenges that an entrepreneur faces as she grows her business relates to a simple yet powerful question: "Toward what end am I growing my business?" In answering this question, an even more foundational question must be answered: "Is growth, in and of itself, a noble goal?"

In the business paradigm of corporate America in the 1900s, bigger was always considered better. When you asked business leaders about how their business was performing, you typically got a response that measured success in terms of sales, market capitalization and/or market share. Many entrepreneurs have been influenced by this perspective, assuming that growing their business as large as the market allows will automatically bring them success. However, there are three aspects to the growth myth that make it a fallacy.

First, the notion of "bigger is better" did not prove to be true for many of the large public companies that dominated the economy during the twentieth century. To continue their growth, many pursued a strategy of acquisition that included buying companies both within their same industry as an attempt to gain more market share and in divergent businesses to aid in financial diversification. However, financial diversification proved to be a strategy that created gigantic but unmanageable corporations. As a result, these same corporations began the process of divesting all business not related to their "strategic core" by the 1980s. And while the acquisitions of companies in their same industry helped gain market share, it did little to stop the long-run decline of these businesses we mentioned in chapter 1.

Second, growth in revenues and market share often do not create more financial success for entrepreneurial ventures. Indeed, growth can be one of the most perilous times for an entrepreneurial venture. As any banker will attest, more businesses fail due to their inability to successfully manage the growth of their company than for any other reason. That is why bankers pay such careful attention to their clients who are experiencing rapid growth. They know the risks that growth can create. The strain on working capital created by increasing inventories and growing accounts receivable; resource needs such as new staff, more equipment and bigger space; the failure to create systems that can manage the increased production of the company effectively; and the failure to delegate can all contribute to failure in a growing business.

Finally, and this is most relevant for building a faithful company, building the biggest business possible often runs counter to the essence of what many entrepreneurs consider to be success. As we saw in the words of entrepreneurs in chapter 2, many define their success in ways that transcend traditional financial measurements like sales growth, increased market share or even profit maximization. They view their businesses as a means to create better places to work and that help build better communities. Although financial success is a desired and necessary outcome to a good company, it is a means, not the end, to building a good company.

Stewardship Practices

While no one practice can prevent the drift we describe above, we have found a variety of practices of experienced entrepreneurs that focus on the efficiency and effectiveness that help a business grow in a mature manner and not simply for its own sake. For the faithful company, these practices take on a new meaning. They are no longer solely the domain of improving the bottom line of the corporation but rather become part of the prudent management of the finite and often scarce resources available to a business.

Bootstrapping, as described in chapter 3, includes a variety of tactics, including various marketing tools, staffing strategies and management systems that allow the entrepreneur to achieve the same ends through the use of fewer resources than might be used in traditional business practices. Bootstrapping offers entrepreneurs tools to make them good stewards of the resources they have been able to attract, including outside financing and employees' labor. The ultimate goal of bootstrapping is to do more with fewer resources. Resources are not squandered for any selfish ends, but rather for the common good of all the stakeholders who have entrusted their money and labor into the hands of the entrepreneur.

Governance structures can be expanded to include a broader representation of stakeholders on both the formal board of directors and informal boards of advisors.

Open book management can be adopted to improve employee access to information and create a better understanding of resource utilization in the business.

Ownership structures can also play a powerful role in integrating stewardship into the culture. When entrepreneurs are too dependent upon outside investors, they can too easily lose control of their companies. When possible, and this is not always the case, entrepreneurs should seek a more diversified ownership structure and bring employees into the structure (see chapter 4).

Identity Drift

The *identity* or culture of an organization is found in the interaction of the various employees, which creates a unique culture or personality in the collective life of the organization. We all know that each organization that we enter has a certain feel to it. If it is a healthy organization, it has created conditions within the workplace that help employees develop. These conditions would include the areas of job design, training and development, compensation, hiring, firing, evaluation, promotion, communication, and so forth. The entrepreneur will design these conditions in such a way that they are informed by the principles on which the company is founded and managed by the virtues she has developed. For the entrepreneurial firm, the *identity* of an enterprise will be heavily influenced by the virtues and principles of the entrepreneur, but also by all those who join the company. How these virtues and principles are articulated and implemented can either contribute to a powerful culture within the organization or one that limps.

In their book *Growing Pains*, Eric Flamholtz and Yvonne Randle examine the challenges faced by all entrepreneurial ventures as they grow, including acquiring resources, developing operational systems and creating management systems. All of these are critical components to the successful navigation of growth. In addition, they view creating an identity or culture that reflects the intended values and beliefs of the founding entrepreneurs to be of paramount importance in building a business that can not only survive the challenges of growth but also thrive in its growth. Good entrepreneurs understand that their enterprise competes as much with their identity and culture as with specific products and services. They know that their problems as a company are more often than not connected to their culture. The enemy is often from within. However, the decisions affecting the culture or identity of a company do not manifest themselves immediately, which can often seduce the entrepreneur into seeing such decisions as unimportant.

Hiring can be one such decision. With all new employees who join a growing business come people who have worked in a different business culture. That culture will have shaped how they act and can shape their values and their character through the work habits they formed in their previous employment.

Those habits do not end when they change employment. New employees will bring remnants of the old culture to a new job. Over time, as more and more new employees join a business, they affect its identity either to the delight or dismay of the entrepreneur.

At the same time, the demands of the day-to-day management of a growing business can lead an entrepreneur to take her attention away from the development of the identity and culture in her business. It is most often not a conscious intent to stray from the original culture, but a case of benign neglect. Together the flow of new employees and the inattention of the founding entrepreneur can lead to *identity drift* in the business. It is rarely a sudden change in culture, but rather a series of slow changes from each small act, each specific decision and each interaction with stakeholders that cumulatively over time can lead to a significant and even fundamental change in culture.

As we saw in the example from chapter 1, Jeff and his partners experienced such a change in his business. After a period of very rapid growth, remember the words of one of his partners: "I hardly recognize this business anymore. It is no longer the kind of place it was when we first started." The culture had drifted away from what they had intended. The change was slow and even imperceptible, but the outcome was clear—the identity had fundamentally changed over the period of about three years of rapid growth.

There are several practices that can help the entrepreneur avoid drift and help build a good culture that will be sustained over time.

Hiring for Culture and Mission

Probably one of the most significant practices of any company's identity and culture is the people it hires. When bringing new people into a business, it is critical to look beyond their technical competence for the position. A fit with the culture and mission of the business should also be examined. Although this can be ascertained through well-crafted, open-ended questions that get at behavioral intent, many entrepreneurs create situational tests to assess cultural fit of prospective employees. Here are two examples:

1. A small service business used the receptionist test to evaluate how possible new hires would fit into their very egalitarian and decentralized culture. In their business, the receptionist was considered a key part of the marketing team, as she had the most daily interaction with employees. She had equal say to the marketing director in the marketing team meetings, where they made decisions by consensus. Prospective employees, unaware of this unique approach, would arrive at the business and would be greeted by the receptionist, and then be escorted back for a series of interviews with key employees. However, the only person who would decide if the applicant would be invited back for a second interview was the receptionist. If she was not treated with respect, she had the sole authority to veto a second interview, no matter how well the rest of the visit went.

2. Just before making an offer to managers, the owner, Robert Ouimet from Tomasso Inc., has what he calls the "dinner with four" meeting. Ouimet and his wife have dinner with the prospective manager and his or her spouse or companion. This is done to get a better sense of the whole person as well as to communicate to the prospective employee the unique project they are about to enter.

Job Design
Job design that is intentionally humane and developmental is a powerful tool in creating and sustaining a good culture. Critical to job design will be the kind of training and development given to employees.

Just Compensation
Just compensation that offers a living wage that is both equitable and sustainable is a fundamental practice in creating and sustaining a strong identity (see chapter 4).

Silence Before Meetings
Many entrepreneurs have implemented the practice of a moment of inner silence and reflection, followed by sharing in meetings of their executive committee and board of directors.

Mission Drift

While the word "mission" is used in different ways, we define it as the way a company impacts the world around it. More specifically, mission will mostly focus on how the organization serves the customer. The mission of the organization is revealed in how it produces or services a "good" that is needed by others. E. F. Schumacher, an economist who was greatly influenced by the Christian social tradition, explained in his book *Good Work* that this missionary function of work enables the person "to overcome his inborn egocentricity by joining with other people in a common task . . . to bring forth the goods and services needed by all of us for a decent existence."[2]

A healthy mission of a company is only authentic when it *serves* the needs of those outside it, which will then serve as a basis of *developing* those within it. The point here is crucial. If a company wants a vibrant and healthy identity that develops those within the company, it has to have a mission that serves the needs of those outside it. We cannot develop as persons unless we are giving ourselves to something outside of ourselves. This is a point that we developed in chapter 1 on vocation.

But for the growing entrepreneurial company, the entrepreneur and her managers can lose that external focus. The demands of managing cash flow, of securing new customers, of managing customers who care only about price, of acquiring needed resources, of meeting new competitive expectations are all examples of the pressures that can take the leadership's attention away from their original mission. The internal needs of the business can quickly draw their attention away from the needs of those outside the business that had been a part of their initial mission. This drift is most often not an intentional decision at a discrete point in time. It happens, almost imperceptibly, one decision, one action at a time as the leadership of the company deals with the parade of crises that most growing businesses must face.

A variety of practices can help keep the mission properly in focus and assure that it serves its intended purpose:

- *Quality of Product/Service*: There are a variety of management tools with a systems-based approach that can help provide critical information about the business and its effectiveness. For example, Continuous Quality Improvement and Six Sigma are two management techniques that strive to minimize defects by empowering managers and employees to make process improvements using data-driven systems. Although not values-based, these techniques can work in conjunction with a mission that is strongly rooted in the entrepreneur's values.

- *Customer Relations*: One of the negative symptoms that can be seen in many growing companies is a deterioration of relations with their customers. This can manifest itself with the loss of long-term customers due to seemingly avoidable problems, a sudden decrease in quality or an inability to fill orders within the proper time frame. Companies such as The Toro Company have instituted programs to directly connect their employees with those who use its products to help them more deeply understand the customer and her needs. In many companies, regular customer surveys and feedback programs to allow customers to provide information about their experience with a business can provide powerful information. Secret shoppers (in smaller businesses these can be people who are friends of the owners; in other cases they are hired by the business) are used by many retailers to provide the business owner with a firsthand perspective from the eyes of a customer. Cross-disciplinary employee meetings, in which staff who regularly interact with customers can share what they hear from those customers with employees who do not have such day-to-day interaction, can also increase awareness throughout a business on the state of customer relations.

• *Environment*: Entrepreneurs may wish to integrate environmental practices into how they intend to operate their business—to make it an integral part of their mission. Each business decision in this context should be examined and reviewed not only for its financial impact, but also in terms of what kind of footprint is being placed on the environment through producing a new product, building a new facility, and so forth.

• *Philanthropy*: Community support and philanthropy as part of a mission statement is another means to connect the business with the outside. Programs such as the paid mission trips in Charles Hagood's company, The Access Group (see chapter 3), are an example of how to institutionalize such actions. Other companies, such as Tomasso, engage in service to the needy, where managers and employees go into the community once or twice a year during paid work time and participate in serving the poor and then reflect together on the experience.

Seeing the Whole

The ongoing challenge for the entrepreneur is to order the stewardship, identity and mission toward the rich vision that often started the company. No amount of technical competency, financial formulas or strategic foresight will make this happen. While these competencies are necessary to successful companies, they are insufficient to making them good and faithful servants. Plain and simple, it takes virtuous entrepreneurs—entrepreneurs who will most likely place less emphasis on a particular business plan with various scorekeeping goals, and more emphasis on building and maintaining a rich, engaging and transcendent vision. It is this vision that must be witnessed in highly principled and virtuous entrepreneurs of the enterprise who can foster respect and a shared sense of vision among the people who join them in their organization.

This is why good entrepreneurs must themselves be witnesses of a vision greater than themselves. All of these *drift* challenges faced by growing companies will test their conviction to this vision. The way the entrepreneur responds to these challenges will reveal whether the virtues are qualities of his soul or merely appearances for show. Jesus is very strong in His warnings on those who do it merely for appearance:

> But take care not to perform righteous deeds in order
> that people might see them; otherwise, you will have no

recompense from your heavenly Father. When you give alms, do not blow a trumpet before you, as the hypocrites do in the synagogues and in the streets to win praise of others. Amen, I say to you, they have received their reward. But when you give alms, do not let the left hand know what your right hand is doing, so that your almsgiving may be secret. And your Father who sees in secret will repay you (Matt. 6:1-4).

Too often Christian entrepreneurs put forward a good show of their apparent virtue as though it is a public relations program. There are few things in Christianity that cause more scandal than hypocrisy disguised as good works. As the great Christian poet T. S. Eliot put it, "the greatest treason, [is] to do the right deed for the wrong reason."

Hypocrisy is not something for us to deny, but to confront. Our colleague Ken Goodpaster tells us we need "to make friends with hypocrisy,"[3] which allows us to realistically and humbly recognize our vices, gaps, divisions, weaknesses and appearances of virtue. This is no easy task in the highly competitive environment of free markets and a pervasively secular culture. But if enough good entrepreneurs can do so in our current entrepreneurial economy, there is hope to build a stronger culture that enables us to pass on the great virtues of prudence, justice, courage and temperance to our children. This will take a great deal of moral imagination on our part and spiritual grace on God's, but the combination will enable us to serve as Jesus did, as a servant who came not to be served, but to serve (see Matt. 20:25-28).

Notes

1. David Specht and Dick Broholm, "Threefold Model of Organizational Life: Testimonies and Queries for Seeing Things Whole," 2001. http://www.seeingthing swhole.org/images/3foldModel.pdf.
2. E. F. Schumacher, *Good Work* (New York: HarperCollins Publishers, 1985), p. 118.
3. Kenneth E. Goodpaster, *Conscience and Corporate Culture* (Malden, MA: Wiley-Blackwell, 2007), p. 154ff.

Selected Bibliography

Alford, Helen, and Michael Naughton. *Managing as if Faith Mattered: Christian Social Principles in the Modern Organization*. Notre Dame, IN: University of Notre Dame Press, 2001.

Aquinas, Thomas. *Summa Theologica*. New York: Benzinger Brothers Inc., 1947.

Aristotle. *Nicomedian Ethics*. New York: Oxford University Press, 1988.

Augustine. *Confessions*. Translated by Henry Chadwick. Oxford: Oxford University Press, 1992.

Brooks, David. "The Organization Kid." *The Atlantic Monthly* (April 2001): 40-54.

Burlingham, Bo. *Small Giants*. New York: Portfolio, 2005.

Flamholtz, Eric, and Yvonne Randle. *Growing Pains* (4th edition). San Francisco: Jossey-Bass, 2007.

Fortin, Jack. *The Centered Life: Awakened, Called, Set Free, Nurtured*. Minneapolis, MN: Augsburg Fortress, 2006.

Gates, Jeffrey R. *The Ownership Solution: Toward a Shared Capitalism for the 21st Century*. Reading, PA: Addison Wesley Longman, Inc, 1998.

Goodpaster, Kenneth E. *Conscience and Corporate Culture*. Malden, MA: Wiley-Blackwell, 2007.

Hardy, Lee. *The Fabric of This World*. Grand Rapids, MI: William B. Eerdmans Publishing Company, 1990.

Heschel, Abraham. *The Sabbath*. New York: Farrar Straus & Giroux, 1995.

Hyde, Lewis. *The Gift*. New York: Vintage Books, 1983.

John Paul II, *Centesimus annus* (1991).

———, *Laborem exercens* (1981).

Kavanaugh, John. *Christ in a Consumer Society, Still*. Maryknoll, NY: Orbis Books, 2000.

Keating, Thomas. *Invitation to Love: The Way of Christian Contemplation.* New York: Continuum, 1995.

———. *Open Mind, Open Heart: The Contemplative Dimension of the Gospel.* New York: Continuum, 2000.

Kennedy, Robert G. *The Good That Business Does.* Grand Rapids, MI: Acton Institute, 2006.

Lubich, Chiara. *Essential Writings.* Hyde Park, NY: New City Press, 2007.

MacIntrye, Alasdair. *After Virtue.* Notre Dame, IN: University of Notre Dame Press, 1984.

Meilaender, Gilbert. *The Theory and Practice of Virtue.* Notre Dame, IN: University of Notre Dame Press, 1984.

Nash, Laura, and Howard Stevenson. *Just Enough: Tools for Creating Success in Your Work and Life.* Hoboken, NJ: John Wiley and Sons, Inc, 2004.

O'Toole, James. *Creating the Good Life: Applying Aristotle's Wisdom to Find Meaning and Happiness.* Emmaus, PA: Rodale Inc., 2005.

Pieper, Josef. *Leisure, the Basis of Culture.* Translated by Gerald Malsbary. South Bend, IN: St. Augustine's Press, Inc, 1998.

———. *The Four Cardinal Virtues.* Translated by Richard and Clara Winston, Lawrence E. Lynch and Daniel F. Coogan. Notre Dame, IN: University of Notre Dame Press, 1966.

Pinckaers, Servais. *The Source of Christian Ethics.* Translated by Sr. Mary Thomas Noble, O.P. Washington, DC: The Catholic University of America Press, 1995.

Salkin, Jeffrey. *Being God's Partner: How to Find the Hidden Link Between Spirituality and Your Work.* Woodstock, NY: Jewish Lights Publishing, 1994.

Schumacher, E. F. *Good Work.* New York: Harper Torchbooks, 1985.

Specht, David, and Dick Broholm. *Threefold Model of Organizational Life: Testimonies and Queries for Seeing Things Whole* (2001). http://www.seeingthingswhole.org/images/3foldModel.pdf.

Stack, Jack. *The Great Game of Business.* New York: Doubleday, 1992.

U.S. Small Business Association Office of Advocacy. http://www.sba.gov/advo/research/.

Yalom, I. "Life in the Balance," *Inc.*, February 1, 1998. http://www. inc. com/magazine/19980201/863.html.

Ward, John L. "Growing the Family Business: Special Challenges and Best Practices." *Family Business Review* 10, no. 4 (1997): 323-338.

Wingren, Gustav. *Luther on Vocation*. Philadelphia: Muhlenberg Press, 1957.

About the Authors

Jeffrey Cornwall is the inaugural recipient of the Jack C. Massey Chair in Entrepreneurship at Belmont University in Nashville, Tennessee, where he is also the Director of the Center for Entrepreneurship and a full professor (visit The Entrepreneurial Mind website at http://forum.belmont.edu/cornwall/). He has held faculty positions at the University of St. Thomas (where he held the Sandra Schulze Chair in Entrepreneurship), The University of Wisconsin-Oshkosh, and the University of Kentucky. In the late 1980s, he left academics to become the Cofounder and President/CEO of Atlantic Behavioral Health Systems, headquartered in Raleigh, North Carolina. After nine years of rapid growth, he negotiated the sale of most of his corporation's business interests, and returned to academics. Previously published books include *Organizational Entrepreneurship*, *Entrepreneurial Financial Management*, *The Entrepreneurial Educator*, and *From the Ground Up: Entrepreneurial School Leadership*. He has received national awards for his work in curriculum development and teaching, and was inducted as a Fellow of the United States Association of Small Business and Entrepreneurship in 2006. Dr. Cornwall consults with a variety of businesses on start-up and growth-related issues. He also consults with larger corporations on reestablishing entrepreneurial cultures within their organizations. His current research interests include public policy as it relates to small business and entrepreneurship and entrepreneurial ethics. He has published numerous articles on various aspects of entrepreneurship, ethics and management. He has a Doctorate in Business Administration and an MBA from the University of Kentucky. He is married with two children.

Michael Naughton is the holder of the Alan W. Moss Endowed Chair in Catholic Social Thought at the University of St. Thomas (Minnesota) where he is a full professor. As a faculty member with a joint appointment in the departments of Catholic Studies (College of Arts and Sciences) and the Ethics and Law (Opus College of Business), he is also the director of the John A. Ryan Institute for Catholic Social Thought, which examines Catholic social thought in relationship to business. As director he has organized international conferences in the U.S., Europe, Asia and Latin America on the theme of Catholic social thought and management, as well as various faculty and administrative seminars on the mission and identity of Catholic universities. His most recent books are *Managing as if Faith Mattered: Christian Social Principles in the Modern Organization*, 2001 (co-author Helen Alford—translated into Chinese, Spanish, Russian and Hungarian), *Rethinking the Purpose of Business: Interdisciplinary Essays in the Catholic Social Tradition*, 2002 (co-editor, S. A. Cortright), *Rediscovering Abundance: Interdisciplinary Essays on Wealth, Income and their Distribution in the Catholic Social Tradition*, 2005 (co-editors, Helen Alford, Charles Clark, S. A. Cortright). Naughton serves on several boards of directors for profit and nonprofit organizations, including the Reell Precision Manufacturing (profit) and The Center for Seeing Things Whole (nonprofit). He is the editor of the series entitled *Catholic Social Tradition* from the University of Notre Dame Press and he serves on the editorial board for the *Journal of Catholic Social Thought*. He received a Ph.D. in theology and society from Marquette University and an MBA from the University of St. Thomas. He is married with five children.